Magic Words

How to Enchant Judges & Conjure Contest Wins

Ellen E. Withers

Scrivenings
PRESS
Quench your thirst for story.
www.ScriveningsPress.com

Copyright © 2025 by Ellen E. Withers

Published by Scrivenings Press LLC
15 Lucky Lane
Morrilton, Arkansas 72110
https://ScriveningsPress.com

Printed in the United States of America

All rights reserved. No part of this publication may be reproduced, stored in a retrieval system, or transmitted in any form or by any means—for example, electronic, photocopy and recording— without the prior written permission of the publisher. The only exception is brief quotations in printed reviews.

Paperback ISBN 978-1-64917-374-4

eBook ISBN 978-1-64917-375-1

Editor: Michael Ehret

Cover by Linda Fulkerson www.bookmarketinggraphics.com

All characters are fictional, and any resemblance to real people, either factual or historical, is purely coincidental.

NO AI TRAINING: Without in any way limiting the author's [and publisher's] exclusive rights under copyright, any use of this publication to "train" generative artificial intelligence (AI) technologies to generate text is expressly prohibited. The author reserves all rights to license uses of this work for generative AI training and development of machine learning language models.

*To writers who want to win contests and see their works published.
Never give up the dream. Never stop learning the craft.
You can do it.*

CONTENTS

Introduction	vii
1. The Importance of Entering Contests	1
2. The Importance of Writing Conferences	7
3. Contest Types and Awards	13
4. Contest Goals	23
5. What Judges Think—Part One	31
6. What Judges Think—Part Two	37
7. What Judges Think—Part Three	49
8. Structure and Sequence	63
9. Setting and Subject	73
10. Plot and Story	79
11. Create a Good Story Arc	91
12. Style and Story	97
13. Magical Characters	105
14. Scenes	113
15. Using Senses and Emotions	119
16. Dialogue	125
17. Quick Checklist for Success	133
18. Embracing the Red Pen	139
19. Professional Editing	151
20. Nonfiction Writing	155
21. Believing In The Magic	163
Glossary of Terms	171
Bibliography	179
Acknowledgments	181
About the Author	183
Also by Ellen E. Withers	185
You May Also Like	189

INTRODUCTION
FINDING THE "MAGIC"

"The greatest gift one human being can give to another is the belief in their own potential."

—Professor Howard Suber

All readers, and most writers, understand there is good magic in a well-written story. If a writer has the proper skills, hones them to perfection, and sprinkles just a little fairy dust over the whole concoction, readers can be transported into another world—a world where time often disappears and new horizons open.

I wrote this book to share some of what I've learned on my long and winding path to publication. I hope the information will shorten your journey to contest wins and publication by helping you reach your goals. With the mastering of many of these skills in contest entry and preparation, you'll be well on your way to realizing your dream.

As a child, I was interested in literature and writing, like many of you. My mother even saved the "books" I created. But, whether it was God's plan, my destiny, or simply meant to be, words and creative writing became a part of my life by a path through nonfiction, technical writing, and magazine editing.

Introduction

The fantastic education I received in these fields was priceless. It opened many opportunities for personal growth.

I wanted to create the magic of stories. I wanted to write mysteries.

Mysteries are like puzzles. And I love a good puzzle. Even my insurance career involved solving puzzles, such as, "How did this fire start?" and "How did this collision occur?" Start with the border—the basic idea that holds the story together. Separate all the like colors, the red herrings, the petty green jealousies, the moody blue characters. And then bring them all together, piece by piece, until you've produced an image of "whodunit" that snares the bad guy and keeps the reader riveted.

Over the years, I improved my skills by attending as many writers' conferences as I could. I also joined the Pioneer Branch of the National League of American Pen Women, a professional organization for writers, artists, and songwriters. Through my association with the local Pen Women branch, I became a board member of the Arkansas Writers' Conference, where I learned the ins and outs of putting on a conference. This provided many more clues, which I'll share here, to creating the enchantment of the written word. In fact, I sowed the first seeds of becoming a published novelist at a writing conference (see more in Chapter Two, The Importance of Conferences). You can do that too.

Along the way, I learned a lot of tricks, spells, and writerly incantations that I incorporated into my writing. Writing may be a solitary endeavor, but getting published is quite the opposite. There is no doubt God had a hand in making my dream come true. He provided a "book village" of people, skilled and supportive, needed to make my first book a reality. It took a lot of work, prayers, and blessings by many people to accomplish this task.

But it also took sharing my writing with the publishing world through entering contests—lots of contests. Almost every contest, even if you don't win, provides the valuable feedback needed to perfect your craft. As I wrote in a blog post for my

Introduction

friend Shannon Taylor Vannatter's website: "The first step to publication is to learn the craft. Figure out what makes a publishable manuscript, and then follow the guidelines. Embrace the fact that you will *always* need to be open to learning. Be an eager student. Immerse yourself in the knowledge and encouragement of those who lecture at writing conferences. I'm grateful to those writers, editors, agents, and publishers who shared their secrets."

After many years of practicing, honing, and improving my writing through contests, conferences, and rear-in-chair dedication, an offer of publication came at the right moment—and it happened through a contest entry.

One day, when the timing was right, and my confidence was high, I took a leap of faith and entered my work in Scrivenings Press's annual Novel Starts contest. That entry caught the publisher's attention, which later led to a book contract.

But how did I craft my spell-binding, contest-winning entry? That's what this book is about. Read on and prepare to learn.

I'm certain there's a contest or two or three—or ten—out there with your name on them. So, faithful wizardly writer, come and learn the things I learned to amaze, enchant, and bemuse editors and contest judges—and *then* learn how to transform that information into contest wins and, hopefully, the opportunity to live your dream.

1

THE IMPORTANCE OF ENTERING CONTESTS

"The ultimate victory in competition is derived from the inner satisfaction of knowing that you have done your best and that you have gotten the most out of what you had to give."

—*Howard Cosell, sports broadcaster*

Short fiction writing contests are the reason I'm now a published novelist. By attending conferences, entering contests, and working my way to awards, I improved my skills. But, because editors and agents also attend these conferences, hearing my name called several times for winning or placing in contests helps them recognize my abilities. Publishers know repeated wins or placements in contests mean you've learned the craft and are mastering the art of storytelling.

Like many of you, I sat down to write "The Great American Novel." I had a desire to write, but to get published, I needed to learn how to produce a product publishers would accept.

There are many reasons for writers of all skill levels to enter writing contests. Beginning writers need the validation that contests give their work. You know you're getting somewhere when you go from no awards to your first Third Honorable Mention.

Experienced writers also need contests to stretch and grow, branching out from their comfortable writing genre from time to time. Creative contests can force experienced writers to stretch the boundaries of their creative minds. A fantastic contest description can provide that incentive—and you might even enjoy the process.

Short fiction contests help you learn to pack a punch in a limited number of words. I am a wordy first-draft writer. Because I know that, I initially write my stories without regard to a word limit.

When I have a completed first draft, I revise for setting, characterization, and plot, still without concern about word count. Then, I revise for the five senses. Do I have smells woven into the tale? Sights described? Sounds that add dimension and depth? Touch and taste by the characters? Will the readers feel the emotions in the story (fear, love, attachment, revulsion)?

Once I've told the story I need to tell, I turn my attention to the word count. If it's too long to enter the contest I've chosen, I save a digital copy of the long version to put away for possible later use. Then I start chopping away at the words.

I start with a critical look at my sentences and phrasing. During my first pass at word reduction, I choose stronger language. Sometimes, an entire phrase can be replaced with one fantastic word.

Here's one secret for you: I can't eliminate all my extra words at once. For me, word reduction works best by removing approximately one hundred words every time I read through it. By the time I've gone through it five or six times—that's a minimum—and cut five to six hundred words, I'm always pleasantly surprised by how much the trimming has improved the story.

Skills learned from contests

Contests teach writers the skills necessary to sculpt a successful career. Abiding by a contest's rules teaches us to respect deadlines. This is the first charm to master. A deadline is a deadline is a deadline. No excuses. No extensions. If we want a publishing contract or a position related to newspapers, magazines, and other periodicals, we must meet deadlines with our best work. You must engrave a deadline on your soul.

In addition to being on time, contests teach us how to conform to expectations. A contest's rules may require us to insert four or five words we would normally not use. Or require a mystery that doesn't have a dead body. Sometimes, they request a Western where there is no shootout. Why? Them's the rules, and the why doesn't matter. (But it's usually to encourage outside-the-box creativity.)

These seemingly arbitrary requirements might initially frustrate you, but I encourage you to embrace the challenges. Such twists and turns teach us to flex our creativity in ways that might impress a judge. Editors, agents, and publishers may suggest a different approach to your story that enhances your overall product. The ability to accept these kinds of suggestions goes a long way toward improving your work and encouraging the possibility of getting published.

The ability to follow *all* the directions of a contest is imperative. You can't win a contest if they disqualify your entry for a rules violation. And at the point of disqualification, no sincerely crafted potion will change the judges' minds. There is no path to success as a published author if you disregard the submission guidelines of your desired publisher.

Besides, contests with creative twists can be inspiring. Dealing with these unusual aspects of a contest enhances our creativity, stretching our writing abilities and leveling up our skills.

Word limits teach us to use more expressive language.

Contests have taught me, a self-proclaimed wordy writer, how to live with this affliction. I've learned to allow my initial draft to have as many words as I want. Once drafted, I happily slice it to shreds. My process is to tell the story first, then self-edit. I don't want to interfere with the creative part of my writing while I'm getting the story down. Editing sharpens my work and reduces the redundancies inadvertently dotting my draft. We'll cover more about the value of editing in Chapters 18 and 19.

Regularly entering contests provides a realistic gauge of your improvement. The more you learn, the better your entries will do.

"Magic" trick: After each contest, study what worked and what didn't work as well for the judges. We all have had stories we love, but no judge has yet to see its merit. That's okay. Go on to something else and save your heart story for later. Not everything will appeal to all judges or your audience. Learn to have thick skin, continue to educate yourself about the craft of writing, and move on.

Contests that offer reviews from editors, publishers, or agents are a great opportunity. If you feel confident your skills will impress professionals, then send your submission. If a publisher or agent believes in your talent, you're closer to realizing your dreams. Many of these contests provide priceless feedback about your work. Entry fees vary, so you may have to limit the number of contests you enter. Choose those that offer you the best value for the entry fee, such as feedback from editors, agents, and publishers.

Most contests charge fees. Some fees are quite high. Considering the time commitment contest judges make, many of the costs are justified. For the writer striving for publication, the benefit of having your work evaluated by judges, publishers, and agents outweighs the costs.

Conferences that provide a publisher or agent as a speaker and include the opportunity for you to pitch your work to these experts should be part of your budget. In writing, "what you know" is vital, but there's no denying that "who you know" can be crucial to accomplishing your publishing dreams. Contests and conferences are an investment in your writing career.

One pre-emptive caution: Research any contest you are considering and avoid any type of scam related to the contest or publishing business. If it sounds too good to be true, it probably is.

When going through the feedback from contest judges, your initial reaction might be to resist their advice. After all, they don't know your story as well as you do. Instead of raising your hackles, step back from that position of pride and consider that working publishers, editors, and agents know what is selling—and what is not.

Rather than dismissing their comments, try them. Make a copy of your original work to retain your brilliance, and then make changes according to the feedback you received.

After you've revised using your judges' suggestions, submit the revamped work to your critique group or a trusted writer friend and get their feedback. In the end, it is up to you whether to accept *anyone's* changes—editor, agent, or trusted friend—but I can vouch for my publisher and the editors provided by the publisher. Every suggestion they made improved my work. Instead of being labeled "hard to work with," become known as a writer who is flexible enough to take coaching.

Another great way to strengthen your writing is by reading other published contest winners. *What did she do right? What can I learn from him? Ooo, look at what she did. I wonder how that would work for me?* Some organizations publish anthologies that include contest winners. Other groups highlight young writers' contest winners, teachers' organizations, and poet societies. Studying winners will help you know what a winning entry comprises and why their entry won.

Takeaway One: Writing contests teach you countless skills. They can help you develop your work to the point agents and/or publishers select it for publication.

Takeaway Two: Contests teach you to be coachable by agents and publishers, to conform to suggestions by experts, and to add creative twists to your work. You will also learn to respect word limits and develop a thick skin in reviews of your writing.

Takeaway Three: Contests validate your writing skills and provide proof of the level of your current skills. They show you where you can yet improve.

Takeaway Four: Impressing a publisher with your contest placements can help you get a publishing contract.

Takeaway Five: Find publications featuring contest winners and study them. Then, incorporate what you've learned into your work.

2
THE IMPORTANCE OF WRITING CONFERENCES

"The more that you read, the more things you will know. The more that you learn, the more places you'll go."

—*Dr. Seuss*

"I am a writer. If I seem cold, it's because I am surrounded by drafts."

—*Unknown*

In the last chapter, you learned that I'm a published author because I attended writers' conferences and learned from them. Let's look at that a little deeper.

The first conference I attended was the White County Creative Writers Conference in Searcy, Arkansas, more than twenty years ago. I chose that conference because it was economical, only one day, and about an hour's drive from my home. What I didn't know about writing at that time could have filled multiple books.

And yet, this conference was a blessing to my life in many ways. The attendees welcomed me and made me feel special, even though I was new to everyone. Now, many of those I met there are my dearest friends and associates. I'm thankful God gave me the willpower to attend.

The door prize I received at that conference was a sure sign. It was a book entitled *Writing for Dummies*. How appropriate. I was a dummy who wanted to learn how to write. I learned two lessons that day: Writing conferences are important, and keep learning. Both are key to the success I've had as a writer.

I also joined Ozark Writers League, an organization for writers that has a quarterly meeting, set up like a writing conference. They have knowledgeable speakers and members who are eager to learn. The dues are affordable, and members come from a multi-state area to meet in Branson, Missouri.

A man wearing an enormous cowboy hat, string tie, and vest was at the first meeting I attended. He was loud and funny. Dusty Richards was a genuine cowboy and a Western author. He wrote more than one hundred books. The Western Writers of America organization awarded Dusty three Spur Awards, and he was inducted into the Arkansas Writer's Hall of Fame. Dusty became a mentor to me, as well as dozens, if not hundreds, of other writers pursuing their dreams.

At conferences, I learned from mentors like Dusty to journal, to read and study books about the craft written by successful authors, and to join a critique group. Those mentors taught me to put in the time *and* to allow my desires to lead me.

Many people say things like they "wished they had time to write" or that they "would write if they just had the time." I believe this shows writing is not a priority to them. My advice to you is to *make* writing a priority. If you want to write, allow it to be important. Don't talk down your desires to yourself or anybody else. Explain to your family and those around you that you *need* to do this. Then do it.

At another conference many years later, I met the owner of a small press, Linda Fulkerson. At that conference, Linda heard my name being called several times as they announced contest placements. Note the placements ran from third honorable mention to first place. She recognized that receiving multiple awards was a good sign I knew how to write.

Later during the conference, she approached me and told me about her company, Scrivenings Press, which sponsored two types of contests. One contest, "Get Pubbed," was for unpublished completed works of fiction, while the other contest, "Novel Starts," was for unfinished novels. I realized I had pieces that would fit the "Novel Starts" criteria. One was an unfinished mystery novel, and the other was a short story that could be considered the first chapter of a historical novel. After the conference, I took a chance and entered both of them in the "Novel Starts" contest, each in a different genre.

I was shocked and thrilled both entries won their genre categories. Those wins allowed me to submit the first twenty-five pages of a manuscript for additional feedback. The judges critiqued my pages and encouraged me to complete either entry into a full-length novel for publication. Eventually, I was offered a three-book mystery series contract. My dream had come true, and it *only* took just over twenty years of work. But, since you're reading this book, you may be able to accomplish your dreams faster.

Dusty Richards once told me, "As long as you write, you need to be prepared to learn something new. Whether it be style, character, verbiage, or something else entirely. Learn a new way to express it or write it and incorporate that into your work. It will keep your writing from becoming stale."

There are many affordable writing conferences out there with experts who can teach you a new technique in plotting, or word use, or a trick to eliminate clichés—and so much more. Many conferences also offer low-cost contests with fun and inspirational contest prompts.

To succeed in this business, you must accept that there's a lot to learn—and then get on about the learning. Experts can only teach you if you attend their presentations. Take notes. Ask questions. Get to know what they are looking for in manuscript submissions. Discover what's selling well and what isn't.

At conferences, you will mingle with editors, publishers and agents—people who make their living in the business of writing. Some conferences have book influencers, sometimes called reader influencers. They offer reviews and critiques of books for their followers through social media and websites.

Best of all, conferences bring writers together. If you have writer friends in attendance, they can help you feel at home at a conference. Not only do you make friends, but you can also have those odd conversations about writing techniques with people who understand. You'll pick up tricks of the trade, share laughs over mistakes made, and recharge your batteries for another span of solitary writing.

I've even received an unexpected book idea at a conference. A judge from a short-story contest I won the previous year approached me at a conference and suggested I could write a book inspired by that winning short story. It was a brilliant idea and used a storyline I'd never thought of pursuing. With help from this contest judge, I have a solid, interesting manuscript idea. Would I have thought of it myself? I doubt it.

Harlan Coben is a best-selling thriller author. His "overnight" success took more than ten years. Harlan's wife agreed to let him give this "writing thing" a try. He was to take care of the house, dinner, and the kids while she supported the family. It was his eighth or ninth published book that got him on a best-seller list. He credits some of his success to attending writing conferences where he learned what he didn't yet know about the craft of writing and publishing. He always gives credit to his wife for being patient with his goal to write, thus giving him a chance to succeed.

Writing awards can give writers media exposure in several ways. The sponsoring entity of the award will have publicity about their winners, which will introduce the winners to a new and extensive audience. If there is an award seal or call out about the award on the cover of the book, purchasers will see this and know it's been vetted and found to be outstanding. Awards will also prompt reviews in various media, which will introduce your work to a wider audience of readers.

Conferences expose you to your tribe

Because of my experience of being mentored, I jump at the chance to mentor others. A friend asked me if I would talk to her friend, who is a writer. She felt her friend needed some guidance with his writing goals. This opportunity allowed me to "pay it forward" in writing mentorship. I received a lot of education, encouragement, and confidence from Dusty Richards. It was a thrill to similarly help another writer.

Writers don't always realize how important the writing community is to their writer's heart and soul. Writing is a solitary business, but it doesn't have to be a lonely one. I would never have developed faith in my writing abilities without the encouragement of others. There is power in making friendships with people who think the way you do.

In my conversation with my friend's writer friend, he related his interest in historical fiction. With both journalism experience and as a Research Fellow for the Air Force Academy, he'd been involved with two book publications. He was looking for more. His self-published book was well-received, even award-winning, but he hoped for a better reception with his current manuscript.

I encouraged him to attend a writing conference. Turns out, he'd never been to one. Here was a man with the discipline, the ability, and the drive to write but without a community of writers with which to share the hard journey of writing. We met at the conference. He was delighted with the friendship offered by other writers, the quality of speakers, and the expert advice he received from an editor. The editor worked for a publisher of historical works and provided great career advice.

Sharing ideas for stories with other writers is beneficial. We all have a unique style, so I don't worry that I'll help someone beat me out of a contest placement. I'll be proud if an idea I gave them helps them win. And the friends I have would be happy for me if an idea they gave me helped me win. That mutual support is priceless.

Don't keep yourself on such a solitary path that you write in a vacuum. Be persistent with your writing, but also seek writer friendships. They are essential food for the writer's soul.

Takeaway One: Writing conferences are a great way to meet people who care about writing as much as you do. Find your tribe there and gain education about the craft.

Takeaway Two: Publishers, editors, and agents attend writing conferences. Many conferences allow you to schedule pitches to agents, editors, and publishers. Some provide contests that are judged by industry professionals. These things are great opportunities to meet these people in person and impress them.

Takeaway Three: Writers need other writers. Although writing is a solitary business, you ought not seclude yourself from other writers. Hunt them down and befriend them. You'll be glad you did.

Takeaway Four: Always try to help a fellow writer to the best of your abilities. Your kindness will be a reward you'll cherish.

3

CONTEST TYPES AND AWARDS

"As a writer, the biggest talent you can have is determination."

—*Jordan Rosenfeld*

Someone asked legendary cellist Pablo Casals why he continued to practice at age ninety. He responded, "Because I think I'm making great progress."

—*Pablo Casals*

Lottery advertisements often say, "You can't win if you don't play." So it is with writing contests. You can't win if you don't enter. Once you start looking for contests, you'll discover there are many out there. Which ones are right for you? I try to identify every option available to me, then sort them out as to expense and the size of the contest. It's easier to place in a smaller contest. But it's also important to place in larger, better-known contests. Also consider what you get for your entry fee. A certificate? Free publicity? Valuable feedback?

Research the market or availability for contests and awards for all types and lengths of fiction and nonfiction works. There are contests for flash fiction, short fiction, poetry, novels, self-published, and traditionally published books, as well as nonfiction books.

Some conferences have contests each year. Depending on the conference, sometimes non-attendees may enter for a fee. Others only allow only attendees to enter. A few of the attendee-only conference contests come without an additional contest entry fee; others add a contest fee.

There are also open contests sponsored by magazines and organizations that publish anthologies and collections. These are usually highly competitive. Many writing organizations, such as American Christian Fiction Writers, genre writing associations, and state-based groups, also sponsor contests and award prizes and honors to their members. Some of these contests allow non-members to enter. Research organizations in the genre or genres you're interested in and see what they offer.

Magazines devoted to writing, such as *The Writer* and *Writer's Digest*, have lists of many contests throughout the year. You can find Writers Digest Writing Competitions at www.writersdigest.com/wd-competitions. The Writer's contests can be found at www.writermag.com/contests.

The *Writers' Market Guide*, produced by Writers' Market, is published annually. They provide information about contests associated with many types of writing. You can find more information at writersmarketguide.com. Also, many larger genres, such as Christian Fiction or Romance Writing, publish market guides with contest information, such as *The Christian Writers Market Guide*.

Find them at https://christianwritersmarketguide.com.

New writers pursuing contest entries for the first time may do best to start with contests sponsored by local writing conferences. Those are typically less expensive, more inclusive to new people, and receive fewer entries than contests on a national scale. Once you can consistently place in local contests, consider branching out to regional and national organizations.

Enter contests you "can't" win

Wait. What? Why would I enter if I can't win?

You can still benefit from the experience of entering a writing contest—even one you won't likely win. I recently entered a national flash fiction contest with a reasonable entry price of $10. There were many others with fees running from $25 to $100. I chose this one because it was a national contest at an inexpensive price.

This contest appealed to me in more ways than price. It also allowed for a minimum of ten honorable mention prizes in addition to first-, second-, and third-place cash prizes. With multiple awards given, there is a slight increase in the chance of at least placing.

When contemplating a larger contest, take into consideration possible contest limitations. Is it a national competition? A world-wide competition? The smaller the entry field, the better your chances of placing. That doesn't mean you should only enter small contests. I think it's best to budget with brains. Allow yourself one or two large competitions, whatever you can afford. Put the rest of your budgeted contest entry money into contests with a smaller amount of entries, such as regional or conference-sponsored contests.

The national flash fiction contest was a wonderful learning experience for me. It pushed me to repurpose one of my humorous short stories and cut over five hundred words to make it work for the contest's word limit.

My hope was the submission's humor would help it stand out in a crowded field, so I edited my original story with the additional challenge of maintaining the humor. It was hard to cut more than five hundred words from a 1500-word piece, but I benefited from practicing my editing skills. As I noted before, for me, it was easiest to eliminate a small number of words each day. When I read the story the day following each edit, I didn't miss what had been removed.

Entering a contest with poor odds allowed me to push the envelope of "safe" submissions. Regardless whether or not it placed, I was a winner from the experience of pushing myself beyond my comfort zone.

Roll the dice and take a chance. Your placement might surprise you, and the skills you gain from the experience will be priceless.

Placing in any contest, local or national, will help develop your credibility as a writer. Agents and acquisitions editors will be more open to submissions from you if you prove you can write well.

Book contests and promotion (via publisher):

Although book promotion is a partnership between the author and the publisher, some publishers set aside funds for contest entries. Large presses may fund entry fees for their well-known authors, but while smaller publishers encourage their authors to enter their works in contests, the publisher may not pay the entry fee. Announcing that a book has been entered in a contest allows for a promotional opportunity. Build your brand by sending announcements about contest placements in newsletters, blogs, and social media to spread the word.

Book contests and promotion (self-published):

There are an increasing number of contests out there for self-published books. Do your research into the price and the eligibility requirements, including the date of publication. Contest wins offer the same promotional opportunities as published books do—but you have to do the promotion yourself or hire a marketer to do it for you. Like traditionally published books, send announcements about contest placements in newsletters, blogs, and social media.

What placing in a contest won't do for you

There are so many benefits to entering contests that it seems silly to talk about what they won't do for you. However, if you don't study and learn from what wins and those who win, you'll spend a longer time improving your writing. We all have demands upon our time. When I committed to becoming a writer, I had a full-time job, a husband, teenagers, and household duties.

It took some insisting, but eventually, my family realized I needed time to write to be happy. They respected that time. I studied the craft of writing whenever I found time to read, usually an hour or two before bed. Whatever you need to do, do it. Make your time to write and study writing as important as everything else in your life. Encourage people around you to respect that time.

But a contest win or placement can't help you if you are averse to accepting others' input on how to improve your work or craft. In historical times, there was reasoning that people could learn a craft or skill through an apprenticeship with a master. Writing is also a craft that can be taught and learned, however, many writers refuse this kind of help, believing their work is "perfect" because a parent or best friend or a supposed deity told them it was.

While I am grateful for any such suggestions for improvement, and I encourage you to be grateful as well, I've met several people who would not accept helpful criticism from peers or from published authors. As a result, they develop reputations as a diva or as someone difficult to work with. If that happens to you, it won't matter how many contest wins or placements you have. Agents and publishers won't want you. Keep a humble and open heart—one that is constantly seeking to learn and improve.

Choose your writing subjects in areas that interest you. Write about your passions. Avoid writing about a subject or in a genre as a business decision. If you chase trends, you'll likely fall behind. You won't be on the cutting edge of the next fad, either, because you're too busy chasing the old fad. But when you write from your passions, your work product improves substantially, because passion flows from your typing fingers onto the page.

Know how to evaluate and enter a contest

Research the contest you're considering entering. Do your homework about what the sponsor expects from entries. For example, if you're entering a Christian contest, make sure your entry is clean. If your work has cuss words, drinking of alcoholic beverages, and gambling, your entry could be disqualified. The judge or judges would disqualify your work as "not to type" or "unacceptable to the guidelines of the contest."

A general search engine for information about writers' conferences and writing workshops can be found at www.shawguides.com. This search engine allows you to search by state, country, or specialty.

Follow the rules

When I'm judging a contest, I'm surprised by entries that fail to follow the rules. Following the rules is the easiest way to get your work in front of a judge's eye. Not following the rules is the fastest way to disqualification. Why would anyone submit something in violation of the rules? I believe the answer is that they don't know what they're doing yet.

Following the rules extends to something as simple as making your payment to the correct entity. For many years, I served as the contest chair of an organization that sponsors a writers' conference and a contest. Our contest rules clearly state how to make payment for contest entries. It is a different name from the conference registration. Two organizations. Two purchases. Two payments. Not brain surgery.

However, each year, one-quarter of the entries I receive are

Magic Words

incorrectly paid. Technically, that is one-quarter of the entries that could be disqualified for failing to follow the rules. My organization is small, and I have corrected the payee line on payments made by check or money order. Larger organizations can't possibly do that and won't forgive such an error.

I recently co-sponsored a contest for a conference where we required a minimum amount of words and a maximum amount of words. Out of all the entries received, only one met the qualification of meeting or exceeding the minimum word requirement.

Instead of disqualifying all the rest, the entries were judged on what they submitted. At the conference, we later learned many of those in attendance had never been to a conference before and were new to writing contests and rules. As judges, waiving the minimum requirement for those entries was the right thing to do. There was no reason to crush the spirit of those new to contests. I hope they all learn to read the rules for next time.

A judge may require a minimum number of words for various reasons. I do it because a 1,000- or 1,500-word entry, no matter how professionally written, doesn't compare to a 2,500-word entry in many areas. Those additional words allow for a richness of description, character development, additional dialogue, situating the reader into the setting, stretching the story arc for more interest or excitement, and coloring the work with artistic and poetic devices. Take the gift of additional words and improve your submission by adding this richness.

Before submitting any contest entry, check each contest you want to enter for the specific rules for that contest. It's not difficult to overlook a requirement associated with a particular contest. I've done it. Some contests have words that must be included. Others require a twist at the end. Perhaps the contest is specific that entries must include a "chase or a hunt" or other specific details.

Not following through on these requirements will—and

should—disqualify any entry without them. Also, check to see if there is a minimum or a maximum word limit and verify you haven't failed to reach the minimum or that you haven't exceeded the maximum. Most judges won't hesitate to disqualify your entry for failing to follow the rules. When you're satisfied your entry conforms to all specific details of the contest, submit it. You could be in the top 75 percent of entries simply by following the rules.

I once received an entry where the author told me her computer wouldn't "do the double-spaced format" we'd requested. Really? If an entrant doesn't care enough to figure out how to format the document properly, why should judges care to judge it? If you're unsure about how to properly format a contest entry, ask a tech-savvy friend for help.

There's a reason for the rules

Skills learned when submitting to contests will translate to professional submissions to publishers. Early in my education about writing and contests, I heard a presentation by an agent about the benefits of entering contests. She said learning to follow contest rules prepares you for the nit-picky guidelines agents and publishers have for submissions. Following the rules in contests teaches you to check, double-check, and triple-check the guidelines for agent and publisher submissions. This is a good thing. Because your submissions are competing against *many* other submissions. Why give them a reason to reject your submission? Make sure your submission conforms to every guideline they have, and you'll be at least one step closer to fulfilling those publication dreams.

Publisher-sponsored contests

Most publisher-sponsored contests provide feedback. The feedback often includes detailed comments and possibly a scale

Magic Words

rating of 1 to 5 or 1 to 10 (spanning from poor to exceeds expectations) in various skills and techniques. Predominant strengths and weaknesses will likely be listed. Other topics discussed and/or rated may include professional impact, story and plot, characterization, conflict, dialogue, and sentence structure.

Receiving this type of feedback is gold. Embrace the suggestions and improve what the judges have noted as "insufficient" or "inadequate." Once completed, you may wish to send your revised contest entry for publication consideration.

Any organization sponsoring an anthology or collection with a selection process can be an avenue to publication. Writers Unite! is a group on the Internet and on Facebook with thousands of members. The group routinely sponsors anthologies that are published on Amazon. They review the submissions, and, if selected for the collection, you can create an Amazon author page and add the anthology to your list of published books. Many writing organizations sponsor anthologies, so research these and consider submitting to them.

Takeaway One: Take pride in your work. Follow every rule and recommendation made by the entity or entities sponsoring the contest.

Takeaway Two: Contests can push you to work "outside the box" or otherwise be creative in new ways. Embrace the creativity of contests and spread your wings.

Takeaway Three: Contests help you create writing goals and teach you how to reach them. Analyze your contest results for areas where you need to improve.

Takeaway Four: Entering contests sponsored by agents and publishers gets your work in front of their eyes. Find opportunities for you to meet agents and publishers or for your work to be seen by them.

Takeaway Five: Contests that provide feedback are gold. Learn to improve your work and resubmit.

4

CONTEST GOALS

"To succeed as a writer, have the tenacity of a brush-eating Billy goat."

—*Dusty Richards, Arkansas Writer's Hall of Fame recipient and three-time winner of the Western Writers of America Spur Award*

In events or contests where one entry fee covers all contests presented or that have a nominal fee per entry, why not enter as many as you can? Your odds of placing are increased, and you may find motivation working toward multiple entries.

If a judge receives numerous entries that all reach a high level of writing, at some point, that judge may employ subjective factors to determine a winner. After you've been entering contests for a while, you may learn what a particular judge enjoys reading. Use this knowledge to your advantage and mold your entry to be in line with what they like.

For several years, I placed in an annual contest where the theme was dancing. My short stories included dancing and leaned toward the romance genre. This told me the judge liked romances. I never knew this for sure, but statistically, my romance-themed entries placed higher in her contest than my mysteries. Either I wrote better romances than other entrants, or she didn't care so much for a mystery.

Some event contests have the same judge year after year. Assess how you've performed for that judge in the past. If you know your judges, you'll be miles ahead of your competition because you can tailor your submissions to fit the parameters and the possible subjective likes and dislikes of the judges.

Here's another helpful charm. Enter contests that limit entries, thus increasing your chances of winning. Some examples of these are contests that require the use of certain words or a specific topic. Often you can tweak an existing piece to qualify for entry in multiple contests. If the requirements are to include a forest, a baseball, and a silk scarf, search for any piece you have written with one of those three things in it. It may be easy to add the other two required items.

Put a spin on the contest topic. Looking at the contest topic from a different angle can elevate your work. With an essay category of "The Most Influential Person in my Life," many entries will be about positive role models. I've judged contests like these.

Therefore, a standout entry may be one about a person who had a negative impact. Because of the negative example set, the writer chose to live his or her life differently. The person described in the story showed the writer how *not* to be. You can imagine how this entry stood out among all the others.

Look also at whether the contest judge has a history of awarding honorable mentions or not. Choosing the contest with the more generous judge increases your odds of placing. And remember, each placement adds to the list of credentials that can make your work more appealing to editors, publishers, agents, and even readers.

Realistically, you may have to walk away from a judge who has never awarded a placement for your work after multiple submissions. No matter how perfect your story might be, judges are subjective, and something about the way you write may not resonate with that judge. It doesn't mean you're "wrong" and the judge is "right." Keep writing and keep improving your craft. The act of writing regularly and reading about the craft of writing will improve your skills.

Contests for judging book-length work can be more expensive to enter than a short fiction contest. It takes days to read and evaluate a book, compared to a few minutes to evaluate an essay or short fiction. Usually, several judges evaluate book-length contests. This increases postage fees if they pass a physical book from judge to judge or will require you to submit more than one physical copy.

However, if you use your entry for media exposure, these contests can pay dividends. If you place in the contest, exposure from the contest sponsor will provide many benefits, including an expanded field of readers, additional followers, and, sometimes, opportunities to present at conferences.

Enter to win by following these suggestions

1. The best way to win a contest is to create appropriate entries. A contest highlighting a family member (mother, favorite relative, etc.) is not a contest about you, it's about your subject.
2. Make sure you're entering the correct type of piece in a contest. Essays are not short stories, and a short story is not an essay.
3. Follow all the rules. Read them several times to ensure compliance, and then check again before submitting your entry.
4. Know your genre. Research the generally accepted parameters of the genre you're entering. Westerns are typically set after the Civil War and before 1900,

with a setting that is west of the Mississippi. With mysteries, there are many types, so ensure your piece will fit within the usual parameters. If the contest rules say, "No dead bodies," the contest sponsor means it.

5. Use the exact format called for by the contest guidelines. Standard is 12-point Times New Roman font, double-spaced, with no extra space between paragraphs, etc. Same for any required cover sheet.
6. When submitting a paper entry, don't handwrite anything on it. If you see a mistake, fix it and reprint that page or your entire piece. If any mistake is spotted after submitting something electronically, try to correct it, but understand that the contest rules might prohibit doing so.
7. Walk away from your work for at least a day or two and then review it with fresh eyes before submitting. This may help you spot a typo or a correctly spelled word that is not the word you intended (hair vs. hare, for example).
8. Short stories must be concise and flow at a faster pace with no room for unnecessary detail or repetition. I find it easier to eliminate the duplication of thoughts or actions *after* I've finished a draft. Editing tightens my work. Look for ways to use active voice and specific verbs when eliminating adverbs and adjectives.
9. Learn the magic of letting go. Nothing is perfect. Craft your entry to "the best I can do right now," and then send it in. Don't beat yourself up about anything you want to change when you read it later. That desire to change it is a sign your writing craft knowledge is improving.
10. Writing is a craft. Get as much training as you can. Study self-help books and attend conferences taught

by those who will enhance your skills. Remember: excellent writing wins contests.

In contests, creativity can be rewarded

Break away from all other submissions to stand out in the crowd of contest submissions. Give judges something they can't put down. Reality. What? Isn't escaping reality why we read fiction? Your fiction has to resonate with the truth to engage your readers. It must reflect what readers experience in their own lives. Reality is relatable.

Think about it. How many perfect people do you know? Add an interesting flaw to your protagonist. It makes that character more real, more human, and more sympathetic.

Heroes and protagonists are typically flawed. This enables readers to identify with them and watch them grow and learn as the story progresses. They can also have a hangup, tic, or limp—the possibilities are endless. Think of the TV show character Adrian Monk, a police detective who, after his wife's murder, develops obsessive-compulsive disorder. These challenges turn your character from a two-dimensional person to a three-dimensional person.

But don't leave all the quirks with your protagonist. In addition to a quirk, your villain/antagonist needs to have at least one redeeming character trait. No one is all bad. Adding a redeeming quality makes that character slightly sympathetic so your readers can relate to a part of his/her motivation.

Can you add a twist at the end of a short story, poem, or essay? This is a fantastic way to please and surprise your readers. An unexpected resolution keeps your reader from becoming bored.

Read talented writers to learn from their skills. For short stories, turn to O. Henry, Shirley Jackson, F. Scott Fitzgerald, Stephen King, Flannery O'Connor, and Ernest Hemingway. These novelists also wrote short stories. Also, be sure to read modern fiction authors within your intended genre. Fiction trends have changed throughout the years, and while we can learn from the classics, what was popular a hundred years ago may not be acceptable in modern fiction. Note how the masters and modern-day bestsellers craft dialogue, settings, and conflict. Also study recent anthologies to learn from current writers and poets.

Get creative with your twist endings if you want to enchant a contest judge. What if your romance has the lovers getting into a fight near the end? This would be unexpected and would add an interesting ending twist, even if they resolve the disagreement by chuckling while arm wrestling. What if your cowboy falls off his horse right before he rides out of town? Maybe his celebration of winning the gunfight got a little carried away.

Be bound by good sense and good taste, but other than that, don't get hung up on fears of what someone might think of your work. You are free to write what you feel. Resist the urge to self-censor your ideas. Perhaps you'll want to tone down your piece in the editing process, but don't shortchange your writing to please others.

Takeaway One: Evaluate contests for cost but also apply strategic thinking. It costs more to enter big contests. Are you more likely to place in a smaller contest?

Takeaway Two: Contest strategy also can involve putting a fresh spin on a contest topic. Try entering with an "out of the box" entry.

Takeaway Three: Follow the rules. Then, be sure to follow the rules. End your entry by following the rules.

Takeaway Four: Check your contest entries for every skill recommended by experienced writers. Adding these skills can elevate your work to winning status.

Takeaway Five: Be creative.

5

WHAT JUDGES THINK—PART ONE

"The art of writing is the art of applying the seat of the pants to the seat of the chair."

—*Mary Heaton Vorse*

The first step to success with contests is to know what the judges want, and what they expect in submissions. If you meet and exceed their desires and expectations, you'll end up one of their top picks.

That's why chapters Five, Six, and Seven will all contain comments from actual short story and book contest judges about what they wanted. This information is gold if you're interested in entering and winning contests. Because you're reading this book and learning what actual judges think, you're way ahead of many writers.

Here is a list of some of the most common concerns expressed by judges:

- "I don't want to see typos." No one should submit anything with a typo in it, but it happens. Reading

your submission out loud is a great way to find previously overlooked errors.
- "Impress me." First impressions are vital. Your opening must be strong. If your opening is not compelling, judges will eliminate you from consideration.
- "Be concise." Avoid using unnecessary or flowery words. Never use a five-dollar word when a fifty-cent word is clear and expresses your meaning.
- "Follow the rules." Don't use a distracting font. Most contests require you to use what they specify. Do that.
- "Punctuation matters." Punctuation mistakes or overuse of punctuation, especially exclamation points, show a writer is new and hasn't learned all the tricks of the trade. More than one or two exclamation points within an entire work of short fiction is too many. Seeing a jumble of exclamation points is my pet peeve as a judge. Make sure your punctuation is correct.
- Don't enter an essay into a short story contest and vice versa. Know what is required by the category.

As much as I recommend you to banish most exclamation points, one or two in your story of five thousand words for drama or to exclaim is acceptable. For example: "Phew! What is that smell?" or "Carla! A snake!"

Some judges have described punctuation using a sewing analogy. "Punctuation is the basting that holds the fabric of language in shape." It has also been described as the traffic signals of language, to slow down and notice this, or to take a detour, or stop. If punctuation is the traffic signal of language, then the exclamation point is the danger sign at the end of the road. Let your dialogue tags and action beats (character gestures) convey the emotion. Good writers craft better ways to guide their reader's understanding of the emotion in their story.

The comma and semicolon can be used in most writing as long as they aren't overused, however, semi-colons are typically not used in modern fiction. Overuse of any type of punctuation can annoy your reader. Commas slow the reader a little and the semicolon somewhat more. Use a semicolon or dash when a comma is too weak, and a period is too strong. They can affect the cadence of your writing, which is why their use is important to understand.

Quotation marks are placed where dialogue starts and stops. Dialogue tags and action beats show who is speaking. In the contest world, follow the basics with quotation marks and leave the dumping of them to those who are famous. When you're famous, you can dump them as well. Pick a style. The Associated Press style (A.P. Style) is used for newspapers and magazines, and the Chicago Manual of Style is used for fiction writing. Be consistent with your use of whichever style guide you use throughout your piece.

As a contest judge, it drives me crazy to see punctuation outside of quotation marks. "Really"? "Yes, indeed, my friend". (It should be, "Really?" and "Yes, indeed, my friend.") Somewhere on earth, this might be acceptable in a style guide, but I suggest you refrain from using an obscure style guide with contest entries. There are many differences between American English and British English. Make sure you use the correct usage for the country of your contest.

In researching this book, I reached out to several experienced contest judges with questions. These judges preferred to remain anonymous.

Q1: If you had to choose between a powerful storyline/plot and perfect grammar, which one is more important to a winning contest entry?

Judge one: "Storyline or plot is vital."

Judge two: "I prefer a powerful story and can forgive a few mistakes in grammar and punctuation, but only a few."

Judge three: "A powerful story will be the winner unless it is riddled with grammar errors. Such mistakes detract from the story and reduce the impact."

Q2: What is the most common error in grammar or punctuation that takes a piece out of contention in a contest?

Judge one: "Run-on sentences. Shorten them, and magic can occur."

Judge two: "Exclamation points. More than one or two per page takes me out of the story."

Judge three: "Simple errors, such as the improper use of their, there, they're; misspellings and run-on sentences. All of these weaken the entry."

Q3. What is the best way for writers to improve their work and place higher in contests?

Judge one: "By improving their ability to expand the

theme of the contest or by adding a twist at the end or including a red herring."

Judge two: "By adding conflict. I also like to be surprised by an ending or a twist."

Judge three: "Writers should flush out their piece to ensure it's cohesive. I prefer a conflict with a resolution that has a clever twist or humor."

Takeaway One: Make sure your submission is free of typos and other mistakes. Proofread your submission several times over several days to spot these mistakes. Read your submission aloud.

Takeaway Two: Start your entry strong and keep it that way. Build tension throughout your plot.

Takeaway Three: Be creative with your submission. Develop an interesting plot and consider adding an unexpected twist at the end.

Takeaway Four: Use punctuation correctly.

6

WHAT JUDGES THINK—PART TWO

"There's no telling how many miles you'll have to run while chasing your dream."

—*Tim Gunn*

In this chapter, we'll hear directly from some top contest judges about what you need to know when entering a contest. These are people on the front lines and in the trenches of contest judging. I asked each of them several questions. See—and study—their answers below.

Q1. What are some things you wish all writers knew about preparing contest entries?

Chrissy Willis:

> "Read the rules carefully and learn what proper manuscript format is. Be sure you rely on more than just a program like Grammarly to edit your work. If the contest provides a word limit, then do not exceed that

limit. Also, avoid using unusual fonts or colored ink—this marks you as an amateur.

"Remember that in most cases, a judge's opinion is just that and may have more to do with how that judge likes the subject matter than how they like your writing. It is not personal and in no way reflects your writing ability. When I entered contests, it was to broaden my scope as a writer. For example, I had read but not written science fiction, so I joined a science fiction short story contest. I won and published the story in a well-known science fiction short story magazine."

Kimberly Vernon:

"If you want to be a writer, make the effort to research the different genres or categories before entering. Don't enter an essay when the contest calls for a mystery, and don't enter a fantasy in a memoir. If you don't know what a sonnet is, look it up. Don't waste the judge's or your own time."

Linda Apple:

"Take the time to review the contest guidelines and follow them. Then, carefully review them before entering to ensure you've dotted all the i's and crossed the t's. I have received entries without a synopsis when they were required. I've even received entries without titles, which would make it hard to acknowledge with a certificate."

Renee' La Viness:

"The rules are not guidelines, they are hard and fast rules to follow. Also, research the definitions of the specific genre or category you're entering so you understand what a cozy mystery is or what an essay is. You are not cheating if you have your story critiqued or edited before you submit it. The whole idea of entering contests is to see how well your story competes with others so you can get some idea of whether it might be ready to submit to a publisher or agent. And just because you won first place in one contest does not mean it's ready."

Ruth Weeks:

"Follow the guidelines. If the word count limit is 1,500, do not send 2,000. Know the genre. As an example, Paranormal is not Sci-Fi or Horror. Submit your entry in a Word Document—yet, again, follow the guidelines."

Susan Page Davis:

"Definitely go over the submission guidelines and adhere to them. Go over your entry several times if it's an unpublished entry. Have someone with fresh eyes read your selection carefully too. It's so easy to miss a minor error in your own work!"

Teresa Wells:

"Know the elements of your genre. Judges look for specific landmarks, and if those landmarks aren't evident, the entry will score poorly. Enter the right category. A big part of winning a contest is showing your knowledge of where your story/entry fits. It shows you've done your due diligence and know your genre.

"Also, know the expected word count for your entry and story. Often, the word count for your novel is expected to be included with your entry. If the count is too long or too short for your genre, it shows a lack of preparation or general knowledge of the craft. It's a red flag to the judge that the writer isn't ready for publication.

"Pay attention to the requirements for the contest. If the requirements are for a one-paragraph blurb, single-spaced, and the first five pages of the novel, submit those things and no more, no less. Know how to properly format a manuscript. When a manuscript is poorly formatted, it often is bumped back to the writer to make necessary changes—and sometimes, the entry is rejected from the contest. It is that important! In publishing, there is one right way to format. Know it—and practice it. Anything different makes you look like an amateur.

"Put deadlines on your calendar, and try not to send your entry at the last minute. Also, calendar the announcements for finalists so you'll be watching for your name. On the day before they announce winners, answer every call, even if you think it's spam. It could be the contest informing you of your win. Check the website for semi-finalists, finalists, and winners. Be professional in correspondence. Don't try to dispute your scores or seek a judge to demand an explanation. Thank you notes are nice to send after the contest is over.

"Be careful with social media posts. Open criticism of contests doesn't make the contest look bad. It makes the writer look bad and might keep you from publishing. The place for ranting is in a personal, private journal. Remember, you are not your scores. Just because you get dismal scores doesn't mean you're a poor writer. It means you have some work to do."

Anthony Wood:

"First and foremost, follow all format guidelines, prompts, requirements, and genre specifics spelled out in the contest. It's the easiest thing an entrant can do to increase her or his chances for a win.

"Second, I wish contest entrants would be careful not to misuse terms and actions that are inaccurate or even inappropriate to a specific genre/style.

"Third, I wish entrants would understand that entering contests is *the* way to learn how to prepare a manuscript for publication. The format or grammar requirements may be a bit different, but those who enter contests realize that submitting their work within guidelines ensures a much better chance of getting published. So, it's not really about winning the contest but rather learning the process of manuscript preparation for publication submission. But, entering a writing contest is certainly a character builder, and it's fantastic practice to keep you on your writing toes."

Q2: What are some rewards of sponsoring and judging contests?

Chrissy Willis:

"I have judged for national and international contests, and the cream always rises to the top. What I mean is that the best story or poem always stands out. What I find difficult is distinguishing between second and third place. Sometimes that can be the difference between a third-place award and an honorable mention.

"When I am judging, I usually go through and read each story. Next, I divide them into piles, putting the rejected stories in one pile and the stories I liked in another. Then, I put them aside for at least 24 hours. I then return to the pile of stories I liked, and my third read-through is to weed out any issues. This is when I double-check for errors and plot holes.

"At this point, I usually have it down to my 'final six.' That is when the real work begins. I use what I affectionately call the 'King Henry VIII' method of judging. If you know your history, you are aware that he had six wives, and he kept getting rid of them one at a time, always looking for someone younger and better than the last one. I take these final six and go over them again, but by now, I have selected the top one (that is the story I can't forget and keep thinking about). Then, after weeding out a couple, I am down to four."

Kim Vernon:

"Reading samples of writing at various skill levels has improved my writing. While reading does a great deal to improve writing skills, reading several similar pieces and comparing the relative level of skill of each enables me to focus on things done well, as well as things done not so well. Often, between two well-written pieces, the decision comes down to personal preference."

Linda Apple:

"For me, it is supporting conferences and giving writers opportunities to advance in their craft. I know many who would like to branch out into other genres, and contests provide them with opportunities to try another genre and receive valuable feedback. Plus, it gives insight into the judging process and why one of my entries is passed over."

Renee' La Viness:

"I get to choose what kind of stories I want to read. Scoring/judging the contests helps keep my editing skills fresh. I am helping authors practice their writing and editing skills. Before judging contests, I had 'Imposter Syndrome.' Like many other authors, I was afraid someone would figure out that maybe I wasn't as good of a writer as they thought I was. When I started judging contests, I learned that my writing was competitive. I wasn't an accidental fake. That helped me grow more secure in my talent and skills."

Ruth Weeks:

"Sponsoring and judging are a way to give back/pay it forward. It can be difficult to find sponsors and judges, so this is my way of helping the conferences that have helped me in the past. It's also given me a greater appreciation and insight into the time and effort required to judge. But, the biggest thing I've learned is that judging is subjective—it boils down to what the judge likes."

Susan Page Davis:

"It helps me hear new voices and give encouragement to less experienced writers."

Teresa Wells:

"Working on the inside of a contest, whether judging or coordinating a category, allows you to see what sticks out to a judge. It also shows how subjective writing is. What one judge likes, another might not. It's all part of the professional writing life.

"As a category coordinator, I learned what is unacceptable in formatting. I didn't know how important formatting was before this role. I could see judges' comments, and even when the genre differed from mine, I picked up on ways to elevate my writing. As a judge, I was given writing rubrics to use with each entry, which took much of the subjectiveness out of judging. Those rubrics helped me with my writing."

Anthony Wood:

"First, I have the privilege of reading some really good—and some not so really good writing—in a variety of genres I enjoy.

"Second, being a mentor at heart, I always invite a co-judge to help me score and place contest entries. It's a great experience to train a new judge and then enjoy watching them go on to judge and sponsor a new contest.

"Third, sponsoring and judging contests allow me to support my writing group and the conferences I attend.

"Finally, sponsoring and judging writing contests lets others know that I care about the growth and advancement of new and budding writers who need good quality experiences to build their confidence and steadfastness so they continue to bloom in the writing growth process. Writing is difficult, and contests toughen up new writers in their defeats as well as encourage them in their wins."

Q3. What are some skills and writing craft features that elevate an entry from the middle of the pack to the top tier?

Chrissy Willis:

"I am always looking for clever writing that does not have a lot of cliches or popular phrases. I want things that are well written with a clear storyline."

Kim Vernon:

"Stories that pack an emotional punch always rise to the top tier for me. Stories with both a plot and a sub-plot show a richness and depth that demand attention. A humorous twist, or just an original and interesting storyline, can outweigh squeaky-clean grammar."

Linda Apple:

"Skillfully written humor is always a big draw for me. However, if the entry doesn't lend itself to humor, I want to sense that the writer is writing to me, for me. The entry is reduced to a bad X (Twitter) or Facebook post if the writer is indulging in a pity party or venting."

Renee' La Viness:

"Polish is usually the top expectation in my contests. Creativity—How far outside the box did you write? I love a creative story that follows the rules and requirements, but it was not the story I expected. Title—A title should fit a story and be unique enough that, in two years, it will remind me of that story, even if I don't remember the whole story."

Ruth Weeks:

"I like humor and wit, however, I can't stand silly humor. Outside-the-box thinking is my favorite. I like an unforeseen twist in the plot."

Susan Page Davis:

"Fresh phrasing; a smooth narrative that uses language correctly and doesn't make me stop and reread to discern what the writer meant; a fresh twist on a topic; a main character I can root for."

Teresa Wells:

"Clean copy always wins. By that, I mean a couple of things. First, little to no grammar or spelling errors. Second, make the reader feel the story by using sensory words. Third, and most important, make every word sing. Use powerful words that paint pictures."

Anthony Wood:

"First, I want well-developed characters that immediately draw me into the action from the beginning of the story.

"Second, the story should capture the reader with a well-thought, killer first line, followed by a great first paragraph, page, and chapter.

"Third, learning to follow the guidelines and specifics of a contest allows the judge to enjoy the read without wading through mistakes. I recently judged a contest in which the best story in the batch of entries was sent to the bottom of the pile because of genre-specific errors and more than twenty-five grammatical errors. It was a writer who submitted a winning story but didn't follow the guidelines. A little bit of editing and fact-checking would have garnered that writer a first-place win. Editing is gold to the writer who wants to win a writing contest.

"Fourth, I like a good surprise, especially at the end. Twists and turns, surprises and unexpected actions keep the judge on the edge of their seat and will certainly bring an entry closer to the top of the pile."

Takeaway One: Research genres and know the standard requirements of any genre contest you enter.

Takeaway Two: Grab the judge at your first line and keep them interested until the end.

Takeaway Three: Consider adding humor or other clever writing to your piece.

Takeaway Four: Surprise judges at your ending. Be creative. Be innovative.

7

WHAT JUDGES THINK—PART THREE

"Amateurs sit and wait for inspiration. The rest of us just get up and go to work."

—*Stephen King*

This chapter will conclude the contest judges' interview and will share the bios of each participating judge.

Q1. List some of your biggest complaints as a judge.

Chrissy Willis:

> "Show, don't tell is the key here. Also, people who try to be cute with colored paper or odd fonts. I also have an issue with writers who don't know basic subject/verb agreement."

Kim Vernon:

"My biggest complaint is getting entries that do not meet the criteria of the contest. Another complaint I have is the constant use of vernacular or dialect. If I have to translate as I read, it distracts from the story."

Linda Apple:

"It depends on which genre I am judging. I usually judge inspirational, children, and nonfiction entries. If it is inspirational, I do not want a Biblical lesson; rather, the truth inferred. And write your entry in such a way that the readers don't feel the writer is condescending or that they are being preached to. Rather, write in such a way that the reader can connect with that truth and be inspired by it. If it is for children, the writer should spend time with children of the age group they target. Please don't write your characters in the way you remember when you grew up. Children today are more advanced for their age, their vocabulary is more mature, and their interests are more expansive than when many of us were children. If it is nonfiction, again, please write in such a way that I am better informed and better after having read the entry. Make me think. It is fine to present a problem, but give me a solution—and encourage me."

Renee' La Viness:

"When a contest has specific criteria (word limits, special theme, etc.), it breaks my heart to see a good writer ignore those boundaries. I remember having to disqualify more than half the entries in one of my contests. Some were very good stories, but the authors either didn't pay attention, or they simply disregarded the rules."

Ruth Weeks:

"Incorrect formatting bugs me. In my experience as a judge, I've learned so many do not follow standard formatting rules, i.e., Times New Roman Font, double spaced, first line of a paragraph indented a half-inch, one-inch margins all around, etc. While I tend to overlook this, I do use it as a tie-breaker. It could mean the difference between winning and losing. Judges tend to look first at things they can disqualify a submission for. Why chance this for not knowing something so simple?"

Susan Page Davis:

"I'm not sure why, but lately, I am seeing more misplaced modifiers and run-on sentences. It can be a great story, but if I have to keep stopping to figure out what the author meant, it doesn't sit well."

Teresa Wells:

"I hate when the contestant has blatantly disregarded the guidelines, especially those writers who expect contest officials to give a pass because the writing is wonderful. It's usually not. Writers who've taken time to learn the craft know how important guidelines are. Pet peeves: improper word usage; italics; bolded words within the manuscript; old-fashioned dialogue tags (she exclaimed); on-the-nose dialogue which doesn't further the plot ("Hi, Pat"; "Hi, Tricia"; "How's your day going?"; "Oh fine, and yours?")."

Anthony Wood:

"First, as has already been said, an entry sent in that ignores the guidelines and requirements will not do well. For example, if a contest calls for a 1,500-2,000 word count, I place to the side those entries that fall short or exceed the requirement. An 800-word short story should not win a 1,500-2,000-word contest. Also, I drop any entry to the bottom of the pile if it misses the mark on the genre.

"Second, too much or unnecessary backstory and/or excessive description will make me set the story down.

"Third, too many dialogue tags lower a piece in the standings. Good writing uses the least amount of dialogue tags as possible. Well-developed characters will be easily recognized in dialogue that includes an occasional action dialogue tag.

"Fourth, I look for good denouement. That is, did the story end well, tie up all loose ends, resolve all conflicts, and leave the judge satisfied that their time was well spent reading the story? Good denouement is the icing on the cake of a good story, and a seasoned judge will spot it quickly."

Q2. What skills did you need to develop to place in contests?

Chrissy Willis:

"Attend writing workshops and learn your craft. Then just jump in and try it. Enter contests in genres you haven't written in or areas you don't normally write. Use contests as opportunities to try something new."

Kim Vernon:

"Be willing to step out of your comfort zone and try to write in other genres. You may be surprised to find you have a knack for writing something you've never tried before. I try to enter as many as I can, as long as the subject is something that interests me. And remember that the results are often subjective. Sometimes, an entry will strike a chord with a judge that no one could have predicted."

Linda Apple:

"Always remember, just because your entry wasn't chosen, it doesn't mean you are a bad writer. It all depends on the judge's personal preferences.

"Losing is hard. I still hate losing. But after the initial pain (especially when I know my entry was inspired, amazing, and the best thing ever written), I must remember that overall, the judge will choose a personal preference. That is one of the great things about judging contests. I am presented with great entries that I must choose the winner from. I try to be unbiased; however, if the entry makes me laugh, think, or inspires me, it is usually the one chosen."

Renee' La Viness:

"Patience. I wanted to be good enough to win first place right away. I started out winning second and third honorable mentions, then moved up to third place and first honorable mention, then slowly up into first and second place. That took a few years, but it was worth the extra effort."

Ruth Weeks:

"I learned that it boils down to what the judge likes. The story might be excellent, and the writing good, but if, for example, the judge is an animal lover, and the dog gets killed in the story, it will not win. I've had to develop a thick skin on this and take any criticism as a learning opportunity."

Susan Page Davis:

"I had to learn to make the main character likable and someone the reader would want to support and cheer on from the beginning. I had to learn not to give all the character's background in the first chapter."

Teresa Wells:

"Hook the reader with the first image. Keep the story moving at an appropriate pace. A low score means I need to learn and keep writing. Contest wins can be so encouraging. But I'll always have to work hard to produce good writing. A win doesn't equal easy street."

Anthony Wood:

"First, learn to develop a "killer" opening line that draws a judge into the story and a fantastic first paragraph/page/chapter that keeps her/him interested. Second, master the guidelines and requirements of the contest. Third, allow readers into your characters' heads. Every reader, especially a judge, should connect with a character in the story, even if not the main character. That way, a judge will become invested in the story. Fourth, tying up all loose ends, ending the story well, resolving all problems and conflicts, and weaving all story threads into a well-woven fabric is essential for a contest win."

Questions related to Book Contests

Q1. Does a book cover influence your evaluation of the book or do you evaluate it solely on the content?

Chrissy Willis:

"It depends on whether I'm asked to judge the whole package or just the content."

Linda Apple:

"Book covers are the flower petals that draw me, but I judge solely on the content."

Renee' La Viness:

"It depends on what the contest organizers wish us to include in the scores."

Susan Page Davis:

"Only if the cover art is extreme in some way."

Teresa Wells:

"As a judge, the cover gives me a first impression, either positive or negative. But the content is what I focus on."

Anthony Wood:

"I've not had the privilege of judging a novel/book contest, but I have experienced several times, at book signings and conferences, passersby and purchasers of my books saying that they were drawn to the covers, which led them to stop and pick up a copy and read the teasers. More than not, they purchased the book. I've also enjoyed purchasers commenting that the content drew them to the book, but that the cover sealed the deal for them. I believe both are critical to the success of a novel or book."

Q2: Any comments you'd like to make about judging full-length books and/or novellas.

Chrissy Willis:

"Full-length books or novellas that don't grab me in the first two chapters don't make the top of the list. Too many authors spend the first couple of chapters with back matter and, frankly, who cares? Start with action."

Linda Apple:

"Judging full-length or novella manuscripts is a true time commitment. I usually read them twice. Before entering a manuscript, have it proofread first. This will keep the judge from being pulled from the storyline. I've judged books where, out of the blue, a character's name is mentioned, and I stop to wonder who that character is, and I go back to the beginning to scan and see what I missed, only to find I didn't miss the mysterious character previously. I'm totally pulled out of the story. Also, and I'm not sure this is the place to mention it, but when there is a scene with only one character, there is absolutely no need to keep repeating that character's name. In this case, pronouns are your friends."

Renee' La Viness:

"It is frustrating to read published books that were not well edited. Some of the most bothersome problems are a lot of typos, not staying in past or present tense, or bouncing back and forth in first, second, and third person. These are very disturbing, even for a reader who doesn't know what is wrong. It just doesn't feel right. These issues are fairly easy to fix if the author will simply take a little time to learn."

Susan Page Davis:

"It takes a big chunk of your time. Don't commit unless you're sure you can handle it without disrupting your schedule too badly."

Judge Biographies:

Dr. Clarissa (Chrissy) Willis:

Clarissa Willis has been involved in early childhood education for more than 30 years. Her experience includes public school, early intervention, curriculum development, and teacher training. As an author, trainer, teacher, special educator, grant administrator, and parent, Dr. Willis offers a unique perspective on early childhood development and special education issues.

Kim Vernon:

Kim has been writing for as long as she can remember. Kim's poetry and short stories have won several local, state, and regional contests, most notably the 2015 Lucidity Ozark Poetry Retreat Grand Prize. Her poetry and short stories have been published in anthologies. *A Rhyme for Every Season*, a collection of her poetry, is currently available. Kim's new book, *A Toolshed Surprise*, was released in October by Lee Press.

Magic Words

Linda Apple:

Born and raised in the South, Linda Apple writes from her soul and speaks from her heart. Linda's novels in her Moonlight Mississippi Series flow from her deep southern roots and the heritage instilled in her since childhood. Because of Linda's respect for her heritage, she also writes nonfiction to help others preserve theirs. Her books, *Writing Life* and *Writing from Your Soul*, are focused on people who do not consider themselves writers. Linda also writes early reader chapter books, *BOWWOW! Book of Winston's Words of Wisdom*, *Winston Learns the Meaning of Christmas*, and *Winston's World, The Way He Sniffs It*. In 2023, Linda was inducted into the Arkansas Writers' Hall of Fame.

Renee' La Viness:

Renee' has been published in books, magazines, newspapers, and anthologies. She has won more than forty writing awards. While editing at 4RV Publishing, she spent two years as the first Children's Corner Imprint Editor. She is the founder/organizer of the annual Meet the Publishers! event in Tulsa, Okla., and a sponsor/judge for multiple writing contests, including the La Viness Short Story Writing Contest. She works as an independent editor and instructor and runs a local writing critique group.

Ruth Weeks:

Writing as R. H. Burkett, Ruth is an award-winning novelist and short fiction author. She's served on the board of the Ozark Writer's League in Branson, Mo., and is a member of the Northwest Arkansas Writers Workshop, Oklahoma Writers Federation, Ozark Creative Writers, Women Writing the West, Mystery Writers of America and Western Writers of America. She has authored or co-authored four books, *Soldiers From the Mist*, *Daughter of the Howling Moon*, *The Rook and The Raven*, and *Broom Flyer's Tales & Spells*.

Susan Page Davis:

Susan is an award-winning author of more than one hundred books. She has garnered many awards during her writing career, including a Carol Award, presented by the American Christian Fiction Writers. She has earned two Will Rogers Medallions and two Inspirational Readers' Choice Awards from the Faith, Hope, and Love Chapter of Romance Writers of America. Three of her books have been "Top Picks" in *Romantic Times Book Reviews* magazine.

Teresa Wells:

Teresa is a former teacher and librarian, who treasures a story threaded with redemption and hope. She is a member of Novel Academy and American Christian Fiction Writers, where she volunteers behind the scenes.

Anthony Wood:

Anthony is a writer from childhood, enjoys researching and writing historical fiction, Westerns, and a variety of other genres, including the occasional poem. He continues to author his series, A Tale of Two Colors, about his ancestor living through the troubled times of the Civil War era. His latest, *The Storm that Carries Me Home*, was released in May 2023, with others soon to follow. In 2024, Anthony was inducted into the Arkansas Writers Hall of Fame.

Anthony's work has been published in *Saddlebag Dispatches*, *The Vault of Terror*, *The Avocet*, and *Winning Writer's Waltz*, an anthology of short stories. His short story, "Not So Long in the Tooth," received a Will Rogers Medallion Award in the Western Short Fiction category. Anthony serves as Managing Editor for the award-winning western magazine, *Saddlebag Dispatches*, as an Associate Editor for Hat Creek, an imprint for Roan & Weatherford Publishing Associates, and as Vice President of White County Creative Writers group.

When not researching and writing, Anthony enjoys roaming historical sites, canoeing, and camping, especially on the Mississippi River, and being with family. Anthony and his wife, Lisa, reside in North Little Rock, Arkansas.

Takeaway One: Avoid traps in your writing, such as using too much vernacular or including too much backstory. Start with action and remove anything that may take your reader out of the story.

Takeaway Two: Learn to be patient with advancing in contests.

You must learn many things as a writer to make it to the top tier of judging. After reaching that level, it's subjective to what a judge wants or likes.

Takeaway Three: Make sure your book is worthy of being judged in a book contest. They can be expensive, and you're wasting your money if you don't have a competitive product. Provide a hook at the beginning, good grammar throughout, an interesting plot, tension, and a stellar ending before considering a book contest.

Takeaway Four: If a book contest includes a book cover, make sure your cover is competitive.

8
STRUCTURE AND SEQUENCE

"A drop of ink may make a million think."

—*Mark Twain*

"I hope someday to write something worth plagiarizing."

—*Unknown*

Your story structure and sequence are important parts of engaging your reader and anyone reviewing your work. Knowing how to use these important tools can give you a leg up when being judged for a contest or determined worthy of publication.

The structure of a story or a book can be deceptively simple. You have a setting with characters, and they experience a conflict. This conflict leads to a climax and then an ending or denouement, which is the conflict resolution. Think of structure as the architectural design of the entire book or story.

There are many excellent resources dedicated to writing structure. My personal favorites include *The Writer's Journey, Mythic Structure for Writers* by Christopher Vogler, and *Story*

Structure, The Key to Successful Fiction by William Bernhardt. Another great resource is *Super Structure: The Key to Unleashing the Power of Story* by James Scott Bell. These educational tools will help you understand how to plan your story's structure. They will also explain the reasons some methods work better for you or appeal to your style more than others.

I use several tools when planning my story's structure. I write a lot of mysteries and use a technique called storyboarding. Storyboarding is the use of note cards, a whiteboard, sticky notes, or digital software to design your storyline. I lay out my storyboarding by scene. Once I'm happy with my sequence of scenes, I divide them into chapters. Some chapters have one scene, while others have several. These options allow for movement and changes, which are necessary for working through a story's timeline and structure.

Mysteries have multiple clues that need to be added, and storyboarding helps a writer decide where to input them. You can also include plot devices such as MacGuffins and red herrings in storyboarding. A MacGuffin is an object or a device that triggers the plot. A red herring is a clue meant to be misleading or distracting to the reader, so they keep guessing as to the genuine mystery.

With most stories, you'll need to determine a timeline. This can be a linear timeline, which is telling the story in chronological order, or by other methods, such as dual timelines.

I wrote my Show Me Mysteries series in a dual timeline, or split time, technique. This means there are two or more timelines where the plot lines intermingle. In my series Show Me Mysteries, each book has a story in the present and a story written in the past. Each era has its characters, so no character is traveling in time.

I move from one era to the other, weaving the story back and forth, which sets up some ebb and flow. I leave a reader hanging in a good way or a mysterious way in one chapter from one era, and the next chapter picks up in the second era. You can intertwine the stories, or have them related to the same setting, or both.

Another term used is time slip, but this differs slightly from dual time or split time. Time slip uses different time eras that are not time travel but the difference is the plot lines of the differing eras don't intermingle.

Time travel is when a character or characters physically move into a different time. The time can be forward, backward, or both, by some type of magical or scientific action.

Research

This may seem elementary but don't write anything without completing research on specific subjects your work will cover. Research the correct details for everything. This means location and setting, terminology related to medical or scientific information, local culture, and dialogue. The Internet is a wonderful research tool, but to have reliable research, you need reliable references.

The best historical references are original source materials, such as diaries and newspapers from the time you're researching. People who lived during the period you're writing about and shared their personal experiences are a treasure of historical knowledge. I like to read historical biographies of important people from the era I plan to write about. They help me get a feel for the times as far as clothing, transportation, and customs.

Librarians are one of the best partners for research materials for any type of research. Research is their life's work, and most love to help their patrons succeed.

Keep in mind you can't transfer all this research onto the pages of your work without putting your readers to sleep. There is a skill at educating yourself as a writer and then flavoring your work with a dash, rather than a shovelful, of information. While research is vital, include too much, and readers will skip it or abandon your book.

Pacing

Avoid having your readers experience a "full run" through your book or story. They need a chance to catch their breath, to think about what you're trying to say. A story's natural ebb and flow is called pacing. Think of pacing as peaks and valleys, highs and lows. However you envision your story, you must have this flow.

Short sentences quicken the pace. Longer sentences slow things down and allow the reader to catch up. The same effect happens when you divide your work into frequent, shorter paragraphs. You can shorten dialogue to increase the pace or to convey aggravation or impatience. A verbal two- or three-word volley emphasizes the feelings of both speakers.

Pacing can revolve around scenes, chapters, characters, and many other techniques. The point is to vary the pace, which keeps your reader and judges engaged. Genres have different pacing. Readers expect a work of suspense to have high tension, divided by some calmer scenes or events. There is a big difference in technique for suspense as compared to writing romance or Sci-Fi.

Flashbacks

A flashback is a memory brought up in time to the story you're telling. Be cautious with flashbacks. They are hard to pull off well, even for a skilled writer. Dropping the information into a conversation or thought in a few sentences is best. A flashback can be lengthy—a scene of its own—or, as with *The Book Thief*, it can be almost the entire book or story. When considering a flashback that is longer than a sentence or two, make sure it moves your current plot forward and is interesting enough to keep your readers engaged.

Aside

An aside is an interruption of your dominant story to communicate an event or events prior to the current scene. Example: "Bobby ran toward the shrubs to hide from his mother, remembering that he'd tried to hide from her about a month ago and that hadn't worked well for him." One way to avoid this is to write chronologically. You can convey what happened "earlier" or "last time" in dialogue when his mother finds him hiding again.

Titles

Wave the flag of your hard work by developing an impressive title. How do you do this?

Determine keywords or the theme of your work, then use a thesaurus to find more words to string together into a clever or compelling title. My mystery series, set in my hometown of Mexico, Mo., has a series title of Show Me Mysteries. Missouri is the "Show Me" state, and because mystery readers seek clues, I felt the "show me" part of the title was a natural fit for the genre.

You can't copyright a title, so you can use a famous title or phrase. Giving it a twist to make it unique could be brilliant. Be creative and ditch overused phrases and titles. Check search engines when you have an idea for a title to see how many are out there in the published world.

Use imagery in your titles. An example of this is *Cat on a Hot Tin Roof* by Tennessee Williams. Readers receive foreshadowing from the title. It clues them into the anxiety, nervousness, and pending uncomfortable situations inside the pages.

Humor can make your titles memorable. Misty Simon has a cozy mystery series with hilarious titles. The first book in the series is *Cremains of the Day*. At the time I heard her speak, she had published fifty-two books, and her publishers accepted her title choices, without change, for all of them.

Excellent titles can be as simple as the subject, such as *Truman* or *Hawaii*. Titles such as *The Devil Wears Prada*, *Everything I Never Told You*, and *How to Win Friends and Influence People* have been selected as outstanding titles in various polls. Other memorable titles include such works as *The Catcher in the Rye*, *Educated*, and *The Red Badge of Courage*.

Staying within the law

Every writer is responsible for his or her content. As the author of this book, I'm sharing my opinions, experiences, and advice with you. I'm not a lawyer. Therefore, I cannot offer you any kind of legal advice. I can offer suggestions based on my experiences and practical knowledge. Any issue in your writing that you believe involves a legal opinion, don't hesitate to contact a licensed attorney who can advise you on that subject.

I have had no experience with a contract associated with any contest I've entered, but some have contracts. Review all the language associated with a contest you're interested in entering. If you have questions, find the answers by contacting the contest coordinator or consulting an attorney. The same advice would apply to a publishing contract. If you don't understand the details, have them explained to you by someone associated with the publishing contract or an attorney.

Plagiarism

Plagiarism is defined as "the appropriation or imitation of the language, ideas, and thoughts of another author and representation of them as one's original work" in the *Random House Webster's College Dictionary*. In simple terms, it means to use someone else's words, works, or ideas and pass them off as your own. It is an honor or ethics code violation. Copyright laws are in place and vary from state to state. Always credit your source materials. By crediting your source, you avoid any question of plagiarism. For further information related to the punishments associated with plagiarism, research your venue.

Random House Webster's College Dictionary defines copyright as "the exclusive right, granted by law for a certain number of years, to make and dispose of copies of a literary, musical, or artistic work." These laws protect those who create original work and give them ownership of that work. Most written pieces of artistic, literary, or musical work have copyright protection for the author's lifetime, plus seventy years. Titles, ideas, and facts are generally not subject to copyright protection.

The U.S. Copyright Office is part of the Library of Congress and maintains records of copyright registration. You can find more information about registering your work at www.copyright.gov. The United States government has been providing copyright protections and services since the Copyright Act of 1790.

Public Domain

We refer to works that are no longer subject to copyright laws as being part of the public domain. This means ownership of the works passed to the general public and no longer belongs to the original artist. Determining whether something has passed into the public domain can be difficult. A check with the U.S. Copyright Office online can tell you when a copyright was registered and if it was renewed.

Fair Use

Fair Use is a term that relates to a judge-created doctrine in United States law. It allows a "limited use of copyrighted material" without having permission to do so from the person or entity that holds the copyright. The U.S. Copyright Office Fair

Use Index can be found at www.copyright.gov. There are four factors used in evaluating a question of fair use. These are found in Section 107 of the Copyright Act:

> 1) Purpose and character of the use, including whether the use is of a commercial nature or is for nonprofit educational purposes;
> 2) Nature of the copyrighted work;
> 3) Amount and substantiality of the portion used in relation to the copyrighted work as a whole;
> 4) Effect of the use upon the potential market for or value of the copyrighted work."

Beware of anything posted on the Internet. The person or organization posting may not have researched and verified that the content they posted is part of the public domain. You should research any use of someone else's materials for copyright issues. It's always best to verify that your right to use the material is legal.

Other laws to research

Privacy laws apply differently to public figures than to your family or neighbor. No federal law at the time of this publication protects a celebrity's right to privacy. If you are considering a nonfiction work, know Federal and State privacy laws and their effect on the people you plan to include in your work. Additionally, be aware that if you publish something false that damages someone's reputation, it could be considered libel.

Takeaway One: Study the methods of how to structure your story. Books and presentations on these methods can help you.

Takeaway Two: Research before you write anything. Learn about your setting, terminology related to any medical or scientific information, and anything related to local culture and dialogue. Add it sparingly to your work.

Takeaway Three: Learn different ways to craft a timeline for your story and determine which method works best for your story or book.

Takeaway Four: Pace is your storyline's peaks and valleys, highs and lows. Develop a pace for your work that allows an ebb and flow that is natural, not boring. There must be natural movement in your story for readers to stay engaged.

Takeaway Five: Recognize that the title of your book or story is as important as the content it contains. Make a statement with a title that resonates.

Takeaway Six: Be familiar with legal issues associated with writing, including copyright laws, privacy laws, and libel.

9

SETTING AND SUBJECT

"A professional writer is an amateur who didn't quit."

—*Richard Bach*

"Great stories are joined to their settings …"

—*Peter Selgin*

Every story needs a strong sense of place. A guaranteed way to give your story that sense is to travel there. But not everyone can pack up and fly to New Zealand or Hawaii, or Qo'noS (home of Star Trek's Klingon race) to get first-hand knowledge of the area. If you can't travel, seek out a similar setting closer to home or talk to people who have traveled to your setting. Then incorporate what you learned into your writing. Alternately, watch YouTube videos or movies or read books set in your locale.

Many writers start with Google to gain the necessary broad strokes of setting. When I was researching hotels in London, I wanted to make sure the area was safe to walk in during the day. Google Maps street view feature of "walking" in the area was fantastic for this. When I used it, I realized it was an amazing writing tool. It gives you the feel of being somewhere, even if you can't get there in person.

For contemporary settings, Google Maps street view allows you to "walk the streets" of your location. I use it to look at buildings, streets, bridges, and other structures.

The websites of museums and historical societies are helpful for grounding yourself in a historical setting. Try contacting museums for a personal visit or a telephone conversation. Most of these places have people who love to assist you with research. Don't forget your library. Public libraries, as well as libraries affiliated with institutions, can provide great magic that will help you place your readers squarely in the middle of your setting.

In general, research into settings online or in person is not for direct use in your story. It's for you to get a feel for the area or subject that is authentic, which will then translate into what and how you write about it.

Once you have some specifics about your subject or setting, consider how your characters or themes might be influenced by the setting. For example, a character in a short story would have completely different challenges in Montana versus New Zealand. There would be climate differences, slang differences, and animal differences. How would things like religion, racial disparities, or cultural differences be different in Big Sky, Montana, versus San Francisco, California? How would your character adapt to or struggle with these differences?

A friend of mine asked me to critique a short story set in a courtroom that involved a criminal trial. In reading her piece, it was obvious she'd seen a lot of courtroom dramas on television and in movies. It was also doubtful she'd ever sat through a real criminal trial, or any trial, for that matter. The difference between real courtroom activities, as compared to television or movie drama courtroom antics, is immense.

Since I have spent many hours in courtrooms for trials and hearings, I could help make her story more realistic. But, I also

Magic Words

learned a valuable lesson. Personal experience with your subject or setting is invaluable. If you don't do enough research, your lack of accuracy will be a giveaway to those more familiar with your setting. To craft a spell that anchors readers—and judges—in your story world, be realistic and faithful to your subject and setting.

But don't overdo it. Include enough, but not too much. Excessive descriptions slow the story and bore the reader. In the past, novelists used more descriptions. There were no computers, televisions, movies, or social media to bring the world into a reader's living room. But today is different, and readers expect fewer details.

Choosing setting pieces that are relatable to everyone can also help. A rainbow, the ocean, or a forest are all things or places to which readers can relate. Most of humanity shares emotions such as grief, frustration, anger, and excitement. Tugging on those known emotions while in a familiar place can make readers relate to your storyline.

Agatha Christie was an expert at settings. One key to her success was using settings she knew, but adding a fictional twist. She set many of her mysteries at country homes and estates—a dark, Victorian setting she was quite familiar with since her sister married the owner of Abney Hall, a grand estate in Britain's Peak District. Her settings employed alcoves, staircases, and even a tunnel that led to the garden.

Christie applied her own experiences and observations to her writing. For instance, she often included the activities of servants in her books. Why servants? No one paid attention to them in real life, and they could get away with fictional murder because they were "invisible."

The mysteries I write involve murder. I have never murdered anyone, but I've been lucky to work with several homicide detectives during my days as an insurance fraud investigator. Knowing the personality of most investigators helps me write with realism.

If you write mysteries but don't know any homicide detectives, find books written by genuine investigators and study what they write. Books and television shows that focus on "true investigations" can be helpful. I try to watch at least one or two episodes of true crime investigation on television each week. I prefer to watch real detectives and law enforcement, rather than a crime drama. When crafting a character, I prefer to base them as much as possible on real people.

If you're writing about a subject unfamiliar to you, try to learn about that subject firsthand. As a mystery writer, I write about guns. My father was a hunter, so I was familiar with rifles and pistols. I've fired both. It was helpful to my writing to know how to clean and load a rifle. I know the difference in the weight of a pistol as compared to a rifle. All this personal experience brings authenticity to my work.

Consider adding some brief history nuggets to make your story richer. To illustrate, my friend's courtroom drama could have benefited from acknowledging the historical presence of all-male juries in the United States until 1937. If your story involves historical weaponry, do you know how heavy the equipment was a century ago? Study how soldiers or Roman gladiators handled their weaponry. Go to a museum and see if they'll allow you to handle a few of their exhibits (with supervision).

Are you using the right words to set the mood of your story? When your setting is in a different era, decade, or country, incorporate a pinch of slang or verbiage from that locale and time. If writing historical fiction or fantasy, these things are critical to establishing the setting and the believability of the setting.

Takeaway One: Know your subject or setting. If not familiar to you, do all the research necessary to describe and incorporate both into your writing realistically.

Takeaway Two: Choose a subject or setting that is relatable to your readers. Readers like places they can relate to as well as characters who are dealing with emotions they are familiar with.

Takeaway Three: When crafting a character, make them and their profession appear real. Base your characters on real people doing actual jobs, but approach it from a fictional standpoint.

Takeaway Four: Consider incorporating some history of your setting into your story to enhance the richness. Adding a small touch of slang and verbiage from that time will make the story more vivid.

10

PLOT AND STORY

"When you're stuck, go back to your characters' motivations."

—*David Mamet*

The definition of plot is simple: Plot is the main events of your story, presented as an interrelated sequence showing cause and conflict. It's the "what" and "why" of your story.

For example, in mysteries, plot might involve solving who killed the victim and why. In a romance, plot explains how two people fall in love. But your plot also tells us *why* these things happened.

A plot, done correctly, comprises a series of scenes that portray a meaning. Each scene is a focused look at something—a precise glimpse of action or conflict that moves the story forward. Some instructors and writers have associated scenes with compartments on a train, all connected yet different, leading to the caboose or the end of your story.

So, plot is simple. What's hard is weaving an interesting plotline throughout your work. Scenes must connect and mesh together to tell a story in words and actions. Over time, characters or situations change, and the plot ends with a climax or some type of resolution to the issues. Many times, characters have opposing goals.

Plot is also concerned with the relationships between the characters. As the reader moves forward in the story, intensity and tension from the character conflict build, and action keeps the reader moving full speed ahead.

Structure (Chapter 8) is the design, the bones, of the story. Plot is the meat on the bones—a fleshing out of the story. When conjuring your plot, ask questions like these:

- What is your protagonist's story goal?
- What conflicts do characters face throughout the story? Plan for conflicts to grow in intensity over the entire length of your story.
- What is the climax of the plot?
- Does your character grow and develop throughout the work?
- If your character doesn't change, what does change? A static story is not of much interest to anyone.
- How is the protagonist's goal resolved?

Determine the central conflict of your story and then decide the major issues your characters will face conflict over. When you've identified this thread or threads, use them as a touchstone throughout the drafting of your story. You should repeatedly address the central conflict through various conversations or internalization. This helps scenes stay connected to the central theme or themes of your work.

Before we get any further into plot, do you know what kind of plot writer you are? There are three general types:

1. The "plotter," who plans or lays out the entire plot, or a large majority of the plot, before writing a single word.

2. The "pantser," who "flies (plots) by the seat of their pants," while writing; and
3. The hybrid writer, who walks the tight wire between the two and does some plotting before they write and some plotting while they are writing.

No matter your approach, your version is correct for you.

"Pantsers" love the fun, surprising journey when telling a story. They rely upon passion and curiosity to provide their inspiration. Knowing it all in advance spoils the fun and may even kill their creativity.

"Plotters" plan things out ahead of time but leave room for changes to be made during the writing process. One of these is not "right," and the other "wrong." Whatever makes you the most comfortable should be the way you create your plot. Be open to changes. Your growth as a writer may change how you plot.

I started as a true "pantser." Although I remain excited about the unknown, I now like to outline/storyboard my scenes before I write them. My comments may be as little as three or four sentences. Sometimes I write the description of the scene when I reach it and not a second before. That's okay. It's more about being comfortable when writing a scene than trying to wedge your creative process into someone else's recommended way.

Subplots

Subplots provide dimension to your story. They increase the interest of your readers and help develop your characters in interesting ways. If you're writing short fiction, you may not have the necessary word count to include any type of subplot. With a longer story, especially novel length, you may want to include one or more subplots.

Readers and judges appreciate the additional aspects of your plot, particularly if the subplots are character-related. For example, your main character has money problems. A subplot could have a relative arrive at the house who couch surfs and eats all the food without contributing monetarily. This serves two purposes. It increases the general tension of the story, and it intensifies the money problem suffered by the main character. Adding these kinds of real-life problems to your characters' lives makes them believable and the storylines richer. Be sure to make a connection from the subplot to your main plot in some creative way.

Story arc

A story arc is the up and down, directional changes, and twists and turns of your story as it unfolds for the reader. Each of these movements is essential to keep a reader interested. Working together, these shifts engage the reader and keep them interested. The more unexpected arcs, the better. We'll look at this in more depth in Chapter 11.

Plot markers or plot points

Plot markers or points impact your characters in irreversible ways. If your plot is humming along Line 1, for instance, a plot marker will shift the tangent to Line 2 or maybe even Line A. These moments impact your character or the direction of the story, shifting potential outcomes. Master these shifts in your story to keep judges from predicting where your story is going. This kind of alchemy keeps readers dialed in.

> **The beginning.** Hook readers with a great opening. Usually, that means action or an emotion—something that pulls them into your story instantly. The trick is to intrigue readers with the information in front of them, moving them to want more. Tease their sense of curiosity

while delivering readers to the place and time of your setting.

How do you want to tell your story? Setting the right tone gives a reader the information they need about what is coming. Is this a comedy? A moody, dark piece? A tongue-in-cheek jest? Set the tone from the outset through the rest of the piece. You are still free to stir in moments that are completely different.

Exposition explains the introduction of characters, the setting, and the ultimate conflict. But be careful, readers can interpret it as "talking down" to them. Too much can dull the story and make it boring. Tell your story with action as much as possible to keep readers engaged.

Action is where you want your book to live. It occurs when something happens that makes or permits something else to happen. Sort of like a domino effect. A killer kills (action), which causes someone to die (action), which causes law enforcement to investigate (action), to solve the mystery of who killed the deceased. Keep the action rolling throughout your work.

Don't ever stop the action to describe something. I was part of a critique group when one of my friends submitted a brilliant scene for review. It was an action scene involving a helicopter firing on the main character and the people he was trying to lead out of harm's way. My friend killed the excitement of the scene when he paused the action to describe the helicopter that was barreling down on the group. He could have described it as "an attack helicopter" or the enemy's "special attack helicopter loaded with deadly missiles and rockets." It wouldn't have slowed the action if he used a few descriptive words. Instead, he delivered too much detail about the helicopter and brought us out of the story.

Rising action is action (and tension) building because of the conflict (which is also building) and the development of characters in your story or novel.

Emotion reels your reader into your story. It lets your readers "see" how your characters react to the problems and issues surrounding them in the story, by showing them the character's emotions. Readers relate to how the characters react to issues—it's almost like reacting themselves.

Conflict has two or more forces grappling with an issue. Robert wants to stay married, but Amy wants a divorce. You can imagine the conflicts that occur with such an issue. Conflict can also be territorial or societal, involving hundreds or thousands of people. The American Civil War is a perfect example of a conflict related to culture, opposing beliefs, livelihood, and more.

Inner conflict means the conflict is entirely within a character. An example might be J.D. Salinger's *The Catcher In The Rye* or Ralph Ellison's *Invisible Man*. Conflict gives your story life and causes your characters to act, feel, change, and develop. Complications also count as conflict. Think of your main character racing out of the house in an emergency only to find a flat tire. Such things increase the dramatic tension and lead to change. Keep your readers guessing about what's going to happen. Keep them thinking, "And then what?"

Hero or Antihero

Your hero must be a role model. If not, you're writing an antihero. Heroes must be good at what they do for a living and have some type of special talent. It helps if they are wounded or imperfect in some way. This makes them a believable hero.

Surprise your readers

Make a list of predictable plot points for your story and then mix in a pinch or two of the unexpected. When I was writing my first mystery, I had a certain person in mind as the killer. Halfway through my first draft, I changed the killer. It ramped up the surprise factor but also added an unexpected twist to a character who previously was weak and uninteresting. I used the haziness of the character to lull readers into dismissing that character as a killer.

Story arc

These are all the directions the storyline takes as it unfolds before the reader. It's the difficulties, the ebb and flow of the action, and the conflicts. They can change direction, slow down, speed up, but whatever you do, keep the reader engaged. A lack of change or fluctuation is boring. (See also Chapter 11.)

Avoid Background Information

Don't bog down your work with historical or background information. Start in the action and sprinkle in the background information a portion at a time, throughout the entire work. It is rare for readers and contest judges to appreciate that background information, but if you incorporate it skillfully, it can be done.

In *For Kicks*, author Dick Francis filled readers in with the background of the main character early, but in an interesting way. He had a secondary character say he'd researched the main character and then offered some of the information. It didn't bog down the story. In fact, it added to the mystique because he left readers wondering why this character researched the main character's background—what was going to happen? This was a perfect blend of information and moving an intriguing plot forward.

Show, don't tell

Study everything you can about how to write with more "show" and less "tell." Contest judges see "telling" with too much frequency, and it's a sure tell (see what I did there?) of the writer's inexperience. Let's look at an example of telling and how to transform it with a couple of flicks of your showing wand.
First example: (telling)

George Hunter drives the wagon home from town. At dinner, he mentions he has to go back to town tomorrow. His father picks up on his nerves and asks why. George looks uncomfortable and hesitates to answer. Eventually, he says it's a business offer.

I know, yawn, right?
Second example: (more showing, less telling)

Upon George Hunter's return home, he unhitched the wagon in the barn and brushed down Clyde before turning him out in their small corral. Maria appeared with a pitchfork of fresh hay.

"I'm sure Clyde would like some feed after taking you to town," Maria said. "Mama says to wash for supper."

Magic Words

"Thanks for the hay. Tell Mama I'll be right there."

"What's wrong? You don't like me calling you in for dinner?"

George shrugged. "Sorry. I've got something on my mind."

At the dinner table, Mama's beans and cornbread seemed to stick in his throat. He glanced around the table to see if anyone noticed. Maria and Mama were chatting about their new neighbors. But Papa took a sip of his coffee and turned his knowing gaze to George.

"Something the matter, son?"

George pushed beans around his plate for a second, then cleared his throat. "Could I get your permission to ride Clyde into town tomorrow? I won't need the wagon, but I need to go back for a bit."

"Why do you need to go again?"

George put down his fork and turned to Papa. "I've been offered a business arrangement. I promised Mr. Dawson he would know my answer tomorrow. Since clouds are rolling in, the weather'll likely be bad tomorrow. I figure that's the best day for me to be gone again."

Papa fingered his coffee cup. "Want to tell me what this is about?"

"Nothing underhanded, Papa." George looked back down at his plate. "I've promised not to say anything until I've brought my answer to Mr. Dawson."

Papa reached for another wedge of cornbread.

"Good of you to keep your promise, son. Clyde is yours for the day. I'm sure whatever you tell Dawson will be the right decision." Then he returned to his meal.

George eyed his Papa as he scraped the remnants of beans from his plate. He prayed he would make the right decision. Especially since he didn't know what was the right thing to do.

Avoid Passive Words

Remove weak, passive words and substitute them with active words. Weak and passive words include was, were, and felt. It is not necessary to remove or reword every instance of these words but make it one of your goals to excise as many as possible. I have a software program that identifies any passive phrases I've missed so I can remove even more of them in the final editing phase.

We've all learned the importance of the first few lines of your work, where you begin casting your spell on the reader or contest judge. It's an invitation for your reader to join the world you've created.

If your beginning grabs a reader and whisks them into your fictional world, then the ending must provide a method to return the reader to reality. It is not enough to close your piece in a satisfying way if you want to impress contest judges. You want your conclusion to capture their imagination and resolve the issues in a fascinating way. You want your ending to live on in their mind long after they've walked away from your work. Be unforgettable, and you'll place in that contest.

I ended one short story with a question. It was a question in dialogue. The immediate issue involving the care of a young orphan was resolved. The story ended with, "Now, what are we

Magic Words

going to do with him?" With that denouement, I invited readers to resolve the future of the orphan in their minds.

Great ways to conjure a satisfying conclusion:

- Resolve all important outstanding issues but imply a (positive or negative) issue to come.
- Make it ring true. Avoid cliché or tricks.
- Don't tell us or show us everything. What is unwritten, but implied, has power.
- Give readers and judges a surprise, something unexpected but not beyond the realm of possibility.

Non-satisfying ending examples:

- If the ending doesn't resolve the story. It just ends because you stopped writing.
- Be more creative than ending with having your protagonist awaken to discover it's all been a dream. It's been done before. On the television show *Dallas*, they brought back Patrick Duffy (after they killed him off a season prior) by showing him in the shower the following season. His wife just "dreamed" the whole prior season when he'd been "dead." The viewing public was furious about this explanation.

Takeaway One: Give your plot a lot of thought before you write. Whether you are a "plotter" or a "pantser" by nature, know where the story starts, where you want it to go, and where it should end. These points can change, but start with a rough idea of where your story is going.

Takeaway Two: Know what plot markers (also called plot points) are. If you plot before writing, lay them out as you expect to use them. If you do not, verify these points are part of your finished draft.

Takeaway Three: Show, don't tell.

Takeaway Four: Craft a fantastic ending with an unexpected twist that rings true and is not a cliché.

11

CREATE A GOOD STORY ARC

"It unfolds as you write it. That's something I never believed before I wrote a book, but it does."

—*Joan Didion*

The plot is the main events of your story, presented by the writer as an interrelated sequence.

A story arc, however, is the up and down, directional changes, twists and turns of a story as it unfolds to the reader. Each of these movements is essential to keep a reader interested in the story. The more unexpected arcs, the better. Judges, acquisition editors, and publishers are all searching for books and stories with believable but unique story arcs.

The goal of a story is the resolution of the plot, with conflicts and complications along the way. Goal examples are: The inexperienced witness to the murder solves the mystery of who killed the victim and why. Or, John and Debbie realize they are or aren't right for each other.

There are as many ways to plot a storyline or story arc as there are ways to tell a story. Here are a few examples, to get you thinking.

Plotting and story arc types

Agatha Christie was one of the greatest mystery writers of all time. She plotted stories in her journals. She would assign an alphabetical letter (A, B, C, etc.) to one of her plot points. Then, she'd list them in various orders until she arrived at the order she wanted.

For example, she might list them as A, D, C, F, E, B, and then try B, A, D, C, F, E, and so on. Her method reminds me of an index card system, where each plot point is written on a card and can be rearranged until the writer arrives at the preferred order. This is an "old school" technique, but it still has merit. Writers who want to see a plot point on something more than a computer screen might like this method. Also, some writers like the feel of the cards in their hands as they shuffle them into the pattern they like best.

Today's writers have many more tools at their fingertips to help with plotting. The digital age brought us software development. Research plotting tools and choose the one that seems the best fit for you.

> **The Three Act Structure:** (beginning, middle, end). This is as simple of a story structure as one can find. There needs to be (1) a beginning that brings the reader into your story. This beginning includes a few descriptions of the setting and/or place. A problem needs to be introduced. The middle (2) shows the protagonist wrestling with the problem. While overcoming that problem may appear impossible initially, the goal of tackling it becomes more reachable as your protagonist moves forward. The end (3) is where your character resolves the problem.
>
> **Story Wheel**: Usually shown as a small circle marked "event," encircled by a much larger circle with pie-

shaped wedges marked "who," "what," "where," "when," "how," and "why." This illustrates all the points that must be addressed in the story.

Scott Meredith's Seven Point Story Plot (1) Character, (2) In a context/setting, (3) With a problem, (4) Character attempts to solve the problem, (5) Repeatedly fails, (6) But finally succeeds, (7) Validation.

Simple Story Outline (1) Introduction: (a) attention grabber, (b) introduce subject, (c) description of feelings, hearing, taste, smells, what you see and hear; (2) Body of story: This is where conflict occurs; (3) Conclusion: Leave the reader with a "kicker" or a "wrap" but leave something to their imagination as well.

Dusty Richard's Plot Example: Dusty was an Arkansas Writers' Hall of Fame author, and in his presentations, he provided a simple layout for novels. He said this example is like a clock: (1) The first 25 percent of the book (or from 12 o'clock to three o'clock), the protagonist is lost. (2) The second 25 percent of the book (or from three o'clock to six o'clock), the protagonist is an orphan, meaning they are alone and have no support for what they must accomplish. (3) The third 25 percent of the book (or from six o'clock to nine o'clock), the protagonist is an emerging hero, meaning they are learning the skills, gathering the knowledge or skills and people to help them accomplish their mission. (4) In the final 25 percent (or from nine o'clock to 12 o'clock), the protagonist becomes a hero or a martyr, which means they right the wrong or accomplish their intended mission—or they die trying.

The Writer's Journey by Christopher Vogler, a screenwriter: Mythologist Joseph Campbell inspired this book. Initially written for screenwriters, this method breaks down character archetypes and then lists and describes the twelve stages of a hero's journey. All types of writers can apply this to their work. The book uses popular movies in the explanation. I highly recommend you add this book and the magic he suggests to improve your story arc and plotting skills.

Multiple Time Periods: The best reference for writing a novel with dual, split-time, or time-slip storylines is *A Split in Time* by Melanie Dobson and Morgan Tarpley Smith. By definition, a split-time novel comprises two or more storylines, typically one in a contemporary timeline and the other in a historical timeline. They can be different characters or the same characters several decades apart.

The stories of a split-time or dual-time plotline intermingle between the past and the present. That means the contemporary story receives clues from the past and won't make sense without the historical part. With time-slip novels, there are different time eras, but the storylines don't intermingle.

Note: Multiple time periods in stories and books are not the same thing as time travel. In a time-travel story or novel, the character or characters travel through time, either forward or backward, or both. The character physically goes to a different era by traveling through time through some construct the author devises.

Takeaway One: A believable and compelling story arc is necessary for your work to keep readers engaged and ultimately win contests.

Takeaway Two: There are several ways to craft a story arc. Study and try some of the different methods to determine which one works best for you.

12

STYLE AND STORY

> "I get a lot of letters from people. They say, 'I want to be a writer. What should I do?' I tell them to stop writing to me and get on with it."
>
> —*Ruth Rendell*

Writers have many choices about how they tell their stories. Let's look at several of those choices and their impact on readers.

Point of view

Point of view, frequently referred to as POV, is the viewpoint of the character telling the story or seeing the story in a scene. It's the person whose eyes are observing and relaying what they observe. Until you are an experienced writer and know the rules and how to break them, stay in one point of view per scene.

Many writers struggle with accidentally changing POV during a scene. The term **viewpoint character** references the head the reader is in during a particular scene or, often, throughout the complete story or novel. Because a character narrates the story, however, this does not automatically make them a protagonist or a major character. Nick Carraway is the narrator of *The Great Gatsby*, but he is not the main character. Think of the viewpoint character as the one the reader is standing behind in the scene. Action happens or is "seen" from their viewpoint.

Point of view types

First-person point of view tells the story from the point of "I." This gives the reader a sense of immediacy about the character who is telling the story. This POV type lets the reader *become* the "I" and "me" through identification with the first-person narrative character.

First-person is an eyewitness account. This point of view is limiting because the scene or chapter or complete work is told solely from the perspective of the one narrative character. Writers must decide who has the most interesting viewpoint in a scene, chapter, or complete work and then write from that character's viewpoint. **Example:** "I watched the couple trading the boy from one car to the other. This brought forward the heartbreak of a broken home."

Third-person subjective point of view is where the narrator is fully experiencing the thoughts and emotions of the point of view character. **Example:** "As she stared at the people pulling the child from one car and shoving him into the other, her heart pounded. She'd learned the fear and heartbreak of a broken home the hard way." This is the most popular choice of action/adventure novelists.

Third-person objective point of view: In this option, your narrator is detached from their emotions and thoughts. **Example:** "She looked at the boy being transferred from one car into the other. She had experienced a broken home as a child." Because of the lack of emotion from this point of view, it is rarely used.

Third-person limited point of view: The narrator tells the story through one character, using he, she, they. In this point of view, the narrator tells the story through only that character.

Third-person omniscient point of view: The narrator tells the story through the eyes of any character chosen, using he, she, they.

Second-person point of view: Telling your story from the point of "you," not you as the author, but a "you" that is one of the characters, or the protagonist, in the story. This is uncommon in fiction, but is frequently used in nonfiction. **Example:** "As you stare at the child being forced from one car to the other, your heart pounds. Experience with a broken home can make you leery of such encounters."

Omniscient: This is an all-knowing narrator or narrative voice that is as distinctive as any character in the story. The omniscient point of view was popular in classic literature but is rarely used in modern fiction. Books that have used this point of view include *Gone with the Wind* and *The Princess Bride*. **Example:** "Laura scanned the parking lot and noted the child being shifted from one car to the other. The sight filled her with dread because she knew what damage a broken home could do."

Tense

In writing fiction, tense is *not* how the author feels as deadline comes whooshing in. In the writing world, tense is a grammatical structure that tells readers when things occur. There are three types of tense:

> **Past**: Events have already happened. Example: "She kissed the cowboy."
>
> **Present**: Events are happening right now. Example: "She is kissing the cowboy."
>
> **Future**: Events haven't happened yet. Example: "She will kiss the cowboy."

So, tenses tell you when the action happened. Tense is important in setting the time frame and perspective of your story and is huge in helping your find your narrative voice.

Choose a tense that works for your story and stay in it.

Present tense is immediate. In present tense, the reader experiences the moment with the character.

Past tense is the most common tense used in fiction, and readers are accustomed to this style. An excellent reference for determining what tense is best for your story is *Spunk & Bite: A Writer's Guide to Punchier, More Engaging Language & Style*. Another general reference is Stephen King's *On Writing*.

Voice

An author's writing voice is something that is developed throughout his or her career. Voice is not how you structure your sentences or the words you choose. Rather, it describes how your soul spills out on the pages of your work.

Voice is based on your personality and your goals. You must

share your feelings with your readers for them to *feel* your voice. The best advice for understanding what voice is and how to develop it is to study the voice of writers you admire and enjoy reading. Study their technique. *True Grit*, written by Charles Portis, is narrated by Mattie Ross, a 14-year-old child. It begins with the narration of a 64-year-old woman, who recounts her adventures in 1878, to avenge the murder of her father. Mattie's voice is an excellent example of how the words chosen, her actions, her feelings, and her motivations expressed, built an unforgettable and unique character.

A great way to practice writing your voice is to write about something you passionately dislike. Because the topic is something you feel strongly about, you will write with confidence and an unwavering stance. Keep practicing this until you are confident you've formed your unique voice out of experience.

Internalization

This is when a character's thoughts are delivered to the reader with an internal monologue. When this technique is used, it allows readers to know exactly what the point of view character is thinking. There are many reasons a character would be unwilling or unable to share these internal mumblings. They can't or won't share these thoughts.

Premise and theme

There can be some confusion between premise and theme. Premise applies when you're generating the idea for your story, essay, or book. Some consider the premise as the idea behind the story. For example: "What if a down-on-his-luck fighter gets the chance to box with a heavyweight champion?" (The premise of the movie, *Rocky*). The premise is formed right at the start of the story when you're developing the idea.

Theme is the underlying message of your work and is woven into the entire piece. Themes are common concepts and are a message conveyed to the reader. They can be subtle, humorous, inferred, or the central topic. In romances, love is the topic, but themes are usually such things as "beauty is in the eye of the beholder," or "a coming-of-age romance between a geek and a cool student" or even "a former love or end-of-life romance rekindled." In mysteries, murder might be the topic, but getting justice for the victim is a common theme.

Tension and suspense

Whatever you write, it must contain tension and suspense. Tension happens within a short period of time, while suspense is a long-lasting effect. Tension can happen when an angry person bursts into a scene. What will they do? What will happen next? An example of suspense is when a child is playing on a playground and disappears when a parent or caretaker is momentarily distracted. So many horrible things could have happened to that child, and a reader's mind runs through those scenarios. Throughout the rest of the work, whether it's a short story or a full-length manuscript, the reader experiences the suspense of searching for and discovering the child.

Readers must have a feeling of uncertainty to remain interested in your work. With romance, the pressure or worry is, "Will these people see they are perfect for each other and fall in love?" In mystery, the overall suspense is, "Can the character or characters work toward finding enough clues to solve the mystery and right the injustice that occurred?" In a genuine work of suspense, readers must feel the constant pull of prospective danger to a character. Experienced authors say, "Send your character up a tree to avoid some type of threat and then throw rocks at them while they're up there." We don't want to throw rocks at our character, but we want to pile on problems for our protagonist to create tension and evoke sympathy from the reader.

Style manuals

A style manual, or style guide, is a set of standards used for the correct formatting of a particular piece of work.

There are several style manuals available to writers, each with a specific purpose. *AP Style*, by the Associated Press, is the English style manual associated with journalism, periodicals, and news writing. *Chicago Manual of Style* is a style guide for English and is commonly used by writers, editors, and publishers of books.

In addition, the *United States Government Publishing Office Style Manual* is used for governmental papers, and *The Christian Writer's Manual of Style* is related to Christian and religious writing. These guides collect the basic rules for the usage of grammar and punctuation in their fields. They also address style questions such as numbers, capitalization, and abbreviations, and much more.

When choosing a style guide to use for your submission, check with the rules of the contest you're entering or with the agent or publisher you're submitting to. If nothing is noted in the guidelines about a specific style required, choose the one you're most comfortable with and follow those guidelines. Don't mix AP Style with Chicago. Choose one and maintain the recommended consistency for that guide.

Takeaway One: How you tell your story depends upon the

choices you make when writing. Learn what choices are available and how they can help or hinder your storytelling.

Takeaway Two: Point of view and tense offer a writer many choices. Research all the options and decide what is best for your current work. You can have chapters that change the point of view and/or tense. Study how writers of renown accomplish this, then try it in your work. Once you've mastered the skill, this is another tool in your writer's toolbox.

Takeaway Three: Developing your writer's voice takes time and patience. Study the writers you feel have accomplished a recognizable voice to learn how they did it. Your voice will come with practice.

Takeaway Four: Every story must have some tension and suspense to make it interesting.

13

MAGICAL CHARACTERS

"Story and characters sell your story as a winner."

—*Velda Brotherton*

Character is derived from a Greek word that means a "distinctive mark." Actors create a character through spoken words and actions. Writers have a toolbox of written words to craft award-winning characters readers will love.

Creating unique characters for your work, whether short fiction or full-length novels, sets your work apart and can make it a winner. There are several ways to design your characters. Some writers prefer to start simply, with a few elements, and flesh out characters as they go. These elements include physical description, actions or goals or external desires, internal desires or unspoken dreams, education, and skills. Once these are in place, then expand on each one.

Other writers develop pages referred to as character sketches. Some have their character write them a letter or answer questions like an interview for a magazine or employment. A few writers have their characters "take" a personality test. My recommendation is to study several options for character development and find one that works for you and your writing process.

Arkansas Writer's Hall of Fame Award recipient Linda Apple speaks to writers' conferences and groups about a clever way to identify character traits. Her presentation is about using elements and the behavior traits associated with them as a basis for understanding yourself as a writer. You can also apply these to character development. Earth, Air, Fire, and Water are the elements highlighted. This information is used here with her permission.

Earth traits are people who are grounded and stable. They don't draw attention to themselves, so you have to "dig" for all the treasure inside them. They are orderly, so they appreciate and honor deadlines. Some of their strengths include their disciplined nature and that they like to do research. Challenges associated with Earth personalities include being perfectionists and the insecurity that goes with it. They also want to give too much information they've uncovered in all that research they do.

Fire people have traits that are bigger than life. They command a room's attention because they are fascinating, bright, and intelligent. They pull others into appreciating what the Fire person is passionate about. It is this intensity and passion that can also put off people. They can come across as condescending and in need of constant adoration.

Water traits are associated with people who are relaxed and thoughtful. Their take on the world can be refreshing to those who need to be uplifted. They are reflective thinkers, always observing but needing solitude to have time to ponder. They can be flexible and conform to a stronger force. Like water, they are stubborn and will not let an obstacle stop their path. They'll just figure out a way to go around it. They tend to find excuses to stay relaxed, so they procrastinate.

Air people are the storytellers. They are expressive and enthusiastic. Because they are great idea people, they can be disorganized and may have messy personal spaces. Organization to them looks like stacks of paper dotting every surface within their reach. They are funny, and this allows them to motivate people and groups. Like the wind they take after, they are unpredictable. Their greatest strength may be their ability to relay a positive and inspiring message.

Make sure your readers have a clear mental picture of each character. Also, each character must be individual, even unique, in their description, dialogue, habits and mannerisms, interests, and background. (See Chapter 16 for dialogue tips.)

I use a spreadsheet for cataloging my characters. It's a great way to keep track of multiple characters, their physical attributes, and quirky traits when writing a book. This helps with a series of novels with repeating characters. The spreadsheet carries over my past information from book draft to book draft, including names, ages, occupations, descriptions, and more.

Write "who" you know. Agatha Christie based Miss Marple on one of her aunts. Christie said her aunt always "suspected the worst in everyone and was usually proved right in the end." She indicated Belgian refugees who came to England to escape German occupation in WWI, inspired the detective Hercule Poirot. They were plentiful and were people "outside" of British society who could perceive things those on the "inside" might not notice. His flaws were also his assets. Christie knew readers become enraptured with an interesting character and remember them.

Clothes are influential for character descriptions and reduce the need for hundreds of descriptive words. Clothing can give you a clue—or mislead you—about a character's economic status. Regional or religious affiliations to clothes are telling, such as what the Mennonite or Amish wear. A cowboy hat or lab coat hints at an occupation.

But keep in mind each unique personality trait when choosing clothes for toddlers, young kids, tweens, teens, college age, middle age, and the elderly. Your fashion-clueless character can wear brown socks with sandals, and you need no descriptive words to further the point you're trying to make. Putting your character (who's having an emotional crisis) taking a shower while fully dressed, placing ice cream in the refrigerator instead of the freezer, or standing outside in a heavy rain shower shows the emotional state of distress or questionable judgment.

Exaggeration is another excellent technique for characterizing. "There I was, towering over her like the Empire State Building." Another example, "He sneered down at this tiny woman in front of him. He could squash her with his big toe. Ten-year-olds were bigger than her." Also, "Waiting for Katherine to appear takes as much patience as watching paint dry."

A character's internal thoughts can be provided to the reader with an internal monologue. This technique, called internalization, allows readers to know what characters are thinking and gives a glimpse of the character's true feelings.

An example:

"Class, I want to introduce Johnny to you. He's joining us from being a homeschooled student."

Johnny looks up at the woman who will be his teacher and frowns. *Does she realize she's thrown me under the bus with all her students? The smirks on their faces tell me everything I need to know about what they think of me being homeschooled.*

Character flaws make them real

To add depth to a character, give them flaws or baggage, both internal and external. It makes them real. We're all flawed, and we, as readers, relate to flaws in characters. Weave these flaws throughout the plot. Don't do a "character flaw" dump. Readers want to see the character reveal themselves, one layer at a time.

The best flaws are when the character's finest characteristic can be a flaw in a unique situation. We all know the very trait you love in someone can be a thorn in your side. An example of this would be a patient character, a man who is calm in a crisis, yet who frustrates his wife because he always runs late. His refusal to sweat the small stuff drives her nuts, yet this trait helps make him the crisis manager she admires.

Character flaws hold your plot together and keep readers interested. As an example, think of Rooster Cogburn in *True Grit*. Rooster would not have been so lifelike and appealing without the loss of one of his eyes and his propensity to drink. Both flaws were believable for a man who had been a soldier in an ugly war.

One of my favorite authors is Michael Connelly. His character sketches are brief on physical descriptions, but he has a way to make their character shine through with their actions and dialogue. Study the works of writers you admire. Not to copy what they've done, but to study how they did it. Note the way they've used their writing skills to accomplish what you admire about their work.

You can describe characters in a few words using several techniques.

- **Actions**: "When the fighting started, Joshua sprinted from the room as fast as an Olympic runner."
- **Exaggeration**: "Paul was built like a fireplug. Dogs must pose a particular threat to him when he's standing outside."
- **Comparison**: "I realized my mistake when he turned to me with eyes like daggers."
- **Physical behavior**: "Harry Truman was known for his habitual smile and calm manner."

Characters must be unique

Each character needs a different personality, one with faults and strengths. Each one's dialogue needs to be as different as they are in personality. These traits, as well as interesting quirks, make readers remember them. They're also relatable because we all have our habits and oddities.

Consider having a character be a liar or a "stretcher" of the truth, an almost unbelievable embellisher. We, as readers, can then be surprised by finding out what they've said is a lie. Or allow the reader to "know" the character is lying, but they're unable to get the message to the protagonist. Either way, the readers will be engaged.

I've had success crafting a character who seems to be nice and unassuming as the antagonist of a mystery. Readers expect the antagonist to stand out somehow, but that's the way authors lead readers down the path they want them to travel. Readers never think "poor Susie" could be a liar and a cheat or a murderess. When revealed to be exactly that, it's exciting for the reader not to have guessed her true character.

Secondary characters can be even more quirky than your protagonist. Sometimes it's better for the way-out-of-the-ordinary personalities or strange quirks to apply to the secondary characters. Your secondary characters should have an interest or "stake" in the story. Also, these characters need to have their desires, problems, and needs beyond their association with the main character or characters. So much so that readers will understand they have "their life" going on beyond the written page.

One of my professors gave me brilliant advice about secondary characters. Have them always do something else until we bring them into the scene. They can be at work or making a sandwich or taking a nap. By having them engaged in their normal activities, then interrupted to provide information or react to what's happening in the scene, they are more realistic to the reader.

Sometimes it's hard to expose your character's underbelly. However, if you don't, they're only paper cut-outs, without the feeling that they're real. We all have emotional baggage we carry throughout life—an embarrassing past, a secret not to be shared, or feelings of guilt and regret. Let your characters have these things because they add wonderful dimension. Readers find the suffering and angst of the characters interesting. Not so much with happiness and joy, other than to hope the characters find them in the end. Everyone can relate to feelings of inadequacy, confusion, depression, etc. This makes characters real.

Detective Adrian Monk is a television character with OCD, phobias, and anxiety. He's an appealing character because he's wounded. The challenges associated with his personality made him a brilliant detective. Sheldon Cooper with *The Big Bang Theory* is another example of a wounded yet brilliant man.

Research into personality types will not go to waste on writers. In short stories, the knowledge of the physical traits of a personality type (wringing hands, superficial charm, or inflated self-worth) would help to develop a character in a few words.

Allow characters, especially your protagonist, to be mystified by a situation. You add drama and emotion if a character struggles to determine what should happen next. We do it, so why don't they? Give them time to develop what their response will be to their current, bewildering situation. After a time of contemplation, they're ready to slay the dragon.

Every character needs to serve a purpose in the story. If they don't, get rid of them. How does the hero find out there's a problem? Why, from the nosy friend of his wife who lives to alert everyone about problems and crises.

All the characters in your story should want something. Using the nosy friend example above, her motivation is stirring the proverbial pot. She likes to be the first to know something bad and then spread the ugly information around and watch people react. Another secondary character example could be the neighbor wanting to borrow a lawnmower. He stumbles into a dead body when he crosses through the hedge dividing their properties.

Have you crafted your characters into well-rounded, three-dimensional believable people? Have you shown physical, emotional, mental, and backstory aspects of your characters? Are they reacting and acting in ways that seem forced or natural to them? Does the antagonist have at least one likable trait? If not, give them one. Make sure you keep bad guys human enough to encourage some sympathy from your readers.

Mannerisms can be a fantastic way to make your characters individuals. Characters can have simple gestures, such as pushing eyeglasses back into place or throwing their head to remove stray locks of hair out of their eyes.

Takeaway One: Craft your characters so they feel real. That means they must have flaws, quirks, hopes, desires, beliefs, and disappointments.

Takeaway Two: Research your characters before you write about them by interviewing them or some other means to get to know them.

Takeaway Three: Determine what each character wants. You'll craft a better character if you know their outward and inward goals to pursue and the dreams they want to accomplish one day.

Takeaway Four: Study the characters you admire created by other writers. Analyze how the authors used their writing skills to craft the characters.

Takeaway Five: Use internalization to allow your readers a deeper understanding of the character.

14

SCENES

"Step out of the history that is holding you back. Step into the new story you are willing to create."

—*Oprah Winfrey*

Novel scenes are the building blocks of a story or novel. Each scene is a focused look at something, a brief glimpse of action, or a conflict that moves the story forward. They are told from one character's point of view. The first lesson regarding scenes is basic—if you never grasp this simple incantation, your writing will not succeed in contests or with publishers.

Each scene needs a beginning, a middle, and an end. These are separate pieces that come together to create the illusion you're writing. Some writers have one scene per chapter. Others have several scenes in a chapter. The way you style your scenes impacts the impression you want to make. The type of genre you're writing can lend itself to how scenes are commonly designed. If you're writing a suspense novel, for instance, you will likely have shorter, edgier scenes written in short sentences. This keeps the pace of the story quick.

Keep in mind that while television, movies, and even video games have faster editing and quick visuals, most readers would not appreciate that fast of a pace throughout your work. There must be an ebb and flow.

Drafting a scene

When you're creating a scene, color code or make a note where the scene begins, what you believe is the middle of the scene, and where the end of the scene begins. Some authors use different color fonts as they write to make this clear. Just remember to change them all back to black before you submit. The notations (or color coding) let you see how you've laid out your scene. This can help you determine if they need to be adjusted.

While in the drafting stage, choose the characters involved in the scene. Once drafted, review the scene to decide if you've gathered the right characters. Could you add more conflict if you added a character? Or took away a character? Or substituted this character for that one? Is there humor added if you insert the grumpy next-door neighbor stopping by to be nosey at just the wrong time?

Once you are satisfied, review the scene to ensure it advances your story. *Each scene must move the plot forward.* If it doesn't, you're slowing down the plot, and the scene needs to be removed regardless of how well-written it is.

Moving the plot forward example: A scene with a confrontation where we see the hidden personality of an important character is good. Especially if readers need to know that previously hidden personality trait.

Failure to move the plot forward example: A confrontation where no clues are revealed, where people agree or argue, but we learn nothing new about their personalities. This scene must go because it's unnecessary.

Magic Words

Pro tip: I never actually delete scenes, but I do remove them, or parts of them, and place them in a folder of deleted scenes. Once it's deleted from the story, it's gone, so that's why I never delete it. When "deleted" scenes are moved somewhere else, you can come back to that scene, or snippet of a scene, later. Saving your discarded work can pay off in less work later. I've had several instances where I've used a deleted (but saved) scene later or have updated a discarded scene to work in a future part of my story.

Have a purpose or goal for each scene. Characters should state or show what they want, so readers understand what's at stake. Other characters should be the naysayers, opposing the action or goal. This adds conflict to the scene.

Another great trick to learn is to let readers experience the unfolding action in a scene. Don't summarize. Moment-by-moment development makes the scene realistic. Readers and judges can feel cheated when you summarize and deny them the unfolding action.

Some of the best scenes involve dialogue between characters. Dialogue provides important information in an interesting way. With dialogue in a scene, the reader experiences the event as an eyewitness to a conversation. It's action, rather than telling. Dialogue keeps the story moving and can give a distinct voice and characterization to your characters. No two people speak the same way, and neither should your characters. (See more in Chapter 16.)

Pace, purpose, and conflict

Pay attention to the pace of your scene. Make sure it fits where you're creating it. An action or suspenseful scene should have a majority of shorter sentences to enhance the tension. Brief paragraphs, too, help keep the quick pace and the reader engaged. A scientific novel would need to provide readers with details related to science. It also needs to touch on the personalities of the characters. A romance often has more words dedicated to character descriptions and personality. Readers want to know the character's outward appearance as well as discover their inner traits.

Here's a more advanced spell, which, if you master it, will help move your writing to the next level. Each scene needs to trigger the next scene, to prepare readers for what's to come. You don't want to write from one cliffhanger to the next. Rather, thread your story in such a way that it naturally leads from one scene to the next. This delivers a structured method of storytelling to your readers.

A great resource for this technique is *A Split in Time, How to Writer Dual Timelines, Split Time and Time-Slip Fiction* by Melanie Dobson and Morgan Tarpley Smith (Ink Map Press). The books highlighted in this guide rely on weaving timelines together. The good news is that the techniques in this book can work in stories that don't involve multiple timelines and can still be helpful to writers who want to improve this skill.

Also, don't forget to have a clear central conflict that is woven throughout the scene and reflected throughout your work. With a romance, the conflict is often whether the main characters will fall in love and figure out how to remain together. In a mystery, the conflict is usually about solving the mystery. Ensure any subplot applies to your overall conflict or purpose of the book.

The end of a scene or a chapter is a good time to have your character worry about what needs to be done or what problems need to be resolved to move forward. This helps keep the reader wanting more and keeps them engaged in the story.

Scene transitions

Narrative transitions can show the passage of time or take the reader to a different place. In a book where you have more than one scene in a chapter, you can use a narrative transition to move from one scene to the other.

Examples related to time are: "Later that night, the cattle seemed settled with no visible lingering effects from the earlier attack." Or "Early the following morning, Sheila cooked breakfast at the stove." Or "Three weeks later, the courthouse appeared deserted, likely because of the upcoming holiday weekend."

Examples related to taking readers to a place are: "In the backyard, the children were playing soccer." Or "Once I was inside the front door, no food was on the table, nor was there any aroma of prior cooking." Or "Three houses down, they parked cars on the grass."

Using a symbol for a scene break is another way to transition. These are indicated by three hashtags, centered, with no spaces between them (###). These symbols and written transitions are necessary to ensure the reader isn't taken out of your story to figure out "what in the world just happened?"

In short fiction, using a limited number of scenes is recommended. Also, take care with point of view, choosing the strongest one, or possibly two, POVs to use throughout the story. Some contest judges will downgrade stories when they feel there are too many scenes for a shorter work of fiction. Some judges believe a short story takes place at a particular time and place, with only one scene.

Takeaway One: Scenes are a mechanism for plotting your story.

Takeaway Two: Analyze your scenes to ensure they move the story forward and create tension and/or action. Include action and dialogue in scenes to engage readers.

Takeaway Three: Weave your scenes together to form a strong storyline and plot.

Takeaway Four: Write clear transitions from scene to scene or chapter to chapter.

15

USING SENSES AND EMOTIONS

"If I, deaf, blind, find life rich and interesting, how much more can you gain by the use of your five senses?"

—*Helen Keller*

"Don't tell me the moon is shining; show me the glint of light on broken glass."

—*Anton Chekhov*

As a contest judge, one short story still stays with me because of the impact it had on me as a reader. The story involved a group of hungry children who were given freshly baked bread. It blew me away when the words on the page made me smell that bread. When you bring your reader into the room where your story takes place, you have a tremendous piece of writing. We connect smells to our memories, and descriptions of smells can pull the reader into the story better than many literary devices.

Incorporating some of the five senses into your writing is an enchantment that can elevate your piece into winning prose.

Well-known romance author Jodi Thomas said, "If I notice a problem with one of my chapters, it's because I've forgotten to add smells, touch, etc."

A good story outline of an introduction of a piece includes: 1) attention grabber; 2) introduction of your subject; and 3) description, which may include feelings, sounds heard, tastes, smells, what your character sees and might reach out and touch or brush past. Using the senses seizes a reader's attention and deepens their interest throughout the story. Readers and contest judges want to experience the story, not just to be told about it.

Descriptions told through the eyes of other characters give readers a visual picture and a clue into that character's personality. A police officer will describe a crime scene differently than a horrified bystander. It's more interesting and possibly more revealing of the horror of the situation to get the description from the bystander. This also allows for dialogue, an exchange between the investigator and the witness, to shape the reader's experience.

Taste details are effective in bringing forward memories and defining character. Examples: "She preferred warm dark chocolate fudge drizzled over her ice cream, but Larry had requested colored sprinkles." Or "His mouth tasted like he'd licked an ashtray."

In just a few words, the sense of touch can show us details about a character. Think of the images you get from the phrase "his sweaty palm" used in a handshake or her "dry skin" during a kiss on the cheek.

Sounds are another sense readers can easily relate to and understand. Creatively mention the slurp of soup or drink, and your reader is magically teleported into the scene. The crunch of a fresh apple, the snick of a lock opening, or a squeak from a porch swing transports the reader to another time and place. Do your best to transport your readers, and you'll find winning contests just became easier.

Incorporating emotion

Emotion is a primal sense, evident within the five senses of touch, smell, sight, sound, and taste. Our emotions and senses are inseparable, often intermingling, offering us hints about the world around us and guiding our emotional responses. Smoke smells can be a warning of fire. The smell of freshly baked apple pie can evoke home.

Such feelings, provided by your character's senses, offer similar information about their environment. The callus-roughened touch of a farmer's hand would differ from the smooth, soft touch of an infant's skin. If a stranger's hands feel coarse during a handshake, your character could jump to the conclusion that this is someone who works with their hands. This creates many areas a skilled writer can inform, or lead astray, his or her reader with sensory details.

Readers and contest judges have to feel connected to your work. They must care about your characters. They need to like or love your characters or at least find them interesting or entertaining.

Of course, "caring about" your characters can also mean negative types of caring: A child afraid of an old man's gruff-sounding voice or a woman's abhorrence at the way a character is acting or has treated someone or a group of people. A well-crafted "bad guy" stirs the reader's negative emotions. They may feel revulsion, a compelling need to stop them from doing more evil deeds, or a desire to bring them to justice.

Adding an unpleasant scent to an antagonistic character lifts the revulsion onto a higher plane. A mention of sour breath or the odor of day-old sweat makes readers react negatively. Readers want to wrinkle their noses in disgust. A character who envelops the world around her in waves of a popular perfume is descriptive of her excessive nature.

Visceral emotions such as feeling gut-punched or being frozen with fear when facing a loaded weapon help the reader feel and experience emotion as well. Your goal as a writer is to get the reader to feel the gun was pointed straight at them as well as your character.

The more emotion your character has invested in the outcome of your story, the more investment a reader or judge will have while reading it. Will they lose everything they own if the bad guy wins? If your protagonist can't escape in time and disarm the bomb, everyone they love will die. Write from the perspective of being right beside your character as they're defusing the bomb. Describing the action as an eyewitness from a safer place loses urgency and immediacy.

Another type of sense often overlooked is the sense of intuition. We all have it, and, if we believe in folklore, women are all blessed with a generous portion at birth. My opinion is that some things attributed to intuition are merely the act of unknowingly reading body language. You observe someone without realizing you're unconsciously picking up the minuscule actions that give clues about the person's behavior or what they are trying to hide. Then your brain assesses that behavior. Our response is visceral fear or concern.

Many of us, myself included, tend to write serious contest entries. There is nothing wrong with serious writing, but humor is very much a part of being human. It's an emotion relatable to everyone. I challenge you to consider adding humor to some of your pieces. Not all of them lend themselves to humor, but those that do could win because you made the judge smile. One of my friends submitted two humorous short stories in a regional writing contest and won both of the highest-esteemed contests.

There are several ways to add humor to a piece without making the storyline silly or fully comical. Using funny words is a great way to add humor. For example, canoodling is one of my favorite words to lighten up a romantic scene. Words like catawampus, nincompoop, whatchamacallit, doohickey, bodacious, and tomfoolery are fantastic examples of immediate humor splashed into your story with one word.

Another way to add humor is through incongruity and exaggeration. For example, an enormous red-headed man wearing a kilt could be afraid of a "wee dog" barking near his toes. His fear, shown to readers and the contest judges through a series of frantic leaps, could be mistaken for, or compared to, a Highland dance. Another bit of humor could be the "rescue" of the large man by a little boy who scoops up the yapping dog with no fear and then waddles back to his mother.

Exaggeration can make important character points with humor. For example, "There I was, towering over her like the Empire State Building, useful for grasping boxes from tall shelves and dusting tops of refrigerators. She, on the other hand, was the pixie embodiment of style, fashion, and grace."

Humorous cozy mystery author Cindy Sample uses a running gag in her mysteries. Cindy loves chase scenes so much, she wanted to incorporate unique chases into her books. She has used backhoes for a slow-motion chase, as well as zip lines, horses and buggies, and other creative modes of travel. Author Janet Evanovich uses a running gag of car destruction in her Stephanie Plum series. Nearly every book has at least one of Stephanie's vehicles being creatively destroyed.

Physical humor can be funny, especially if most of us can relate to it. Who among us hasn't had some type of fall where we were more concerned about who witnessed the fall than any injury sustained? Relatable humor, where we can laugh at ourselves as well as a character, might win the heart of a judge. Don't wait for a humorous contest to spice your work with a bit of comedy. A piece of work enhanced with a sprinkle of humor can stand out from the crowd and garner you extra points.

Takeaway One: Incorporating senses in your writing brings your reader into the room where your story takes place. For example, descriptions of smells can pull the reader into the story better than many literary devices.

Takeaway Two: Emotion is a primal sense, interwoven within the five senses of touch, smell, sight, sound, and taste. Learn to write about the senses and have a character react in an emotional, primal sense.

Takeaway Three: Add visceral emotions to your characters, such as being frozen with fear when facing a loaded weapon. This helps the reader feel and experience the emotion along with your character.

Takeaway Four: Add humor to your work and make your readers and a judge smile.

16

DIALOGUE

"As far as I'm concerned, 'whom' is a word that was invented to make everyone sound like a butler."

—*Calvin Trillin*

"Don't say the old lady screamed. Bring her on and let her scream."

—*Mark Twain*

We can define dialogue as a conversation between two or more people. In writing, these conversations take place within scenes and can provide important information in a much more interesting manner than a writer telling the reader. Dialogue, in the hands of a brilliant writer, helps the reader experience the event as an eyewitness. Dialogue keeps the story moving. It also gives a distinct voice and characterization to your characters.

Each character in your story should have a unique voice. This includes accents, speech patterns, pauses, and things of that nature. Some people have words they repeatedly say, and this can help define their character if you incorporate it sparingly into dialogue.

One of the best examples of differences in dialogue is to think of what men say as compared to women. Women are the first to jump out and apologize, whether or not they've done or said anything wrong. It's how we calm down a situation. "I'm sorry this has happened to you." Or "Oh, girl! I'm so sorry." Men are famous for responding in monosyllables, especially when confronted by someone upset. "What?" or "Something wrong?"

If you struggle to write dialogue or find that what you've written is stiff and unrealistic, try this dialogue drafting exercise. Place yourself *in* the conversation while you're drafting it. Determine how your characters will respond. Review your goal for the scene. Then, ask yourself how you would respond. Add yourself as an additional character and write your responses as you draft the character's responses.

When completed, review the full conversation. Focus on the dialogue marked as "you." Could you add some of your responses to the intended characters? Would it make it flow better or sound more realistic? If so, add it. If not, there's no loss. Delete the dialogue attributed to you and see what's left. It might surprise you how realistically it flows because you imagined yourself as a part of the conversation.

Another option is to read the dialogue of your characters out loud. Sometimes, speaking the dialogue helps you correct issues. Do you need to incorporate gestures, such as stomping a foot or showing someone gritting their teeth? Are sensory issues missing, such as sounds? Consider adding someone drumming their fingers on the table or shuffling their feet in impatience. Remember to choose movements that fit each character and are not cliché.

Emotions are a huge part of developing the voice of the character and keeping the interest of the readers, including those judging your work in a contest. Filling your characters with believable emotions makes them come alive. Show these emotions within scenes with dialogue. Have them laugh, get angry, and cry.

The best examples of good dialogue I can find are in playwriting. With no real backstory to give audiences, plays show the differences in characters through words and gestures. Storytellers need to read plays. I love anything written by Neil Simon because I "get" his humor and admire his talent. In *The Odd Couple*, he's taken a wide range of characters sitting at a table playing poker and given them all unique dialogue and gestures. He offers a glimpse of history of each character in dialogue. For example, there is a scene when Oscar tells Felix how difficult he was to be married to, and that's why he's divorced. It doesn't ramble on forever. It informs us, in a fun way, that Felix's former wife was a saint in putting up with him for as many years as she did.

Dialogue can increase the speed of your story. Resist the urge to use dialogue to "lecture" the reader or "spill history" into the piece. The best dialogue is direct and goal-oriented, which means the dialogue helps push the story forward. Good dialogue is also brief. We can create an effective verbal argument between two characters with a minimum of words. For example:

Character One: "My hard work has made your life easy."
Character Two: "I resent that."
Character One: "I do too."

Another gift given by dialogue is that it reduces passive voice from your work. Passive writing places your reader at a distance. For example:

General Description: *A rooster was crowing while Mary Lou was visiting a rural area. (passive) She turned to Bob. "I beg you, tell me we are not walking into some barnyard."*

Spoken in dialogue: Mary Lou: "Was that a rooster?" (active—we know she heard it.) She turned to Bob. "I beg you, tell me we are not walking into some barnyard."

During the editing process, review your dialogue and explore the possibility of incorporating a gesture instead of a response. It's more interesting to your reader to imagine the gesture and the reason behind it than to read the words. For example:

Bob didn't answer. He looked at the ground and kicked the dirt.

Dialect or vernacular, along with dialogue, can breathe life into your story and make it shine, though too much can hinder the story. Sprinkle in one or two words, and the reader will know the dialect is there, but they won't have to "translate" the oddly spelled words related to the dialect. It's best if you can use the proper spelling but incorporate a phrase associated with dialect. Regional terms, slang, or even foreign terms mixed into your dialogue can also bring atmosphere and realism to your story. The phrase, "That dog won't hunt," or referring to a soft drink as either "pop" or "soda" or "sodie" or "Coke" gives the reader a geographic clue in the story.

Ozark phrase examples: "Might could" or "I were" rather than "I was." Such small additions to your story can add depth to your characters through dialogue.

British phrase examples: "Put that in the boot." (trunk) or "Shall we take the lift?" (elevator)

Example of a Southern female talking to the police, "Can y'all come in a plain car or something? 'Cause this makes me look like I'm talking to the police, and I don't want to be caught up."

Don't use too much dialect, as it can be annoying and slow down your reader. Just mix it in, here and there, to show a bit of character and background.

Magic Words

Dialogue tags such as "he said" and "she said" become redundant if your dialogue or gestures allow the reader to know who is speaking without using them. You can't eliminate all dialogue tags because that can leave your readers in a state of confusion about who is speaking. A unique voice for each character will also allow you to eliminate some dialogue tags.

Like regional or geographical considerations, a character's occupation also impacts the words they use. A farmer and a geologist will describe the same land with different words. Dialogue should tell us things about a person and things about the story.

Take care to avoid having a character perceived as being "preachy," unless that's the trait you're trying to show. You can say, "He droned on." Or "The preacher rambled in his sermon. The boys frowned at each other, then shifted in their seats as the preacher turned a blind eye to the shuffling of the crowd."

Does your dialogue breathe life into your characters and storyline? Make sure the characters have the proper responses to events with their words and reactions. Are they shocked into silence? Angry? Laughing about what was said?

Things to think about when reviewing dialogue: How does what's said in a scene contribute to character or plot advancement? Is the dialogue natural? Can readers or judges differentiate the characters by their dialogue? Do you have too much or not enough? Remember that pauses, time to ponder, and other delays in speech or replying are part of the dialogue and are important in character development. The same goes for habits that buy time for the responder, such as pushing back their hair, cleaning their glasses, etc.

If your pages aren't filled with dialogue or action, fix them. Many times I draft my scene with a paragraph that is "telling" and then fix it so that it "shows" instead.

Example of an initial paragraph written as "telling:" "Max has moved into town from Rush Hill. Their farm has expanded to acreage in east Mexico. Most of the brothers are now working the newer farm."

Here's an example of conveying the same information through dialogue-based description. This conversation takes place between the main character (Liesl) and a renewed acquaintance (Max) at a birthday party:

"A new home?"

"More like a bunkhouse of brothers. The family bought a cattle farm near town, and four of us boys are living there now."

"Without killing each other?"

He grinned. "We have our moments, but so far, so good."

"A new farm is exciting."

"That's nothing to seeing you tonight." He offered a hand. "Care to dance?"

No character should speak more than four sentences at a time. It becomes an information dump if a character carries on and on. Keep dialogue as "back and forth," mindful of maintaining the reader's attention.

With dialogue, the important parts are not always the spoken words. The drama can be how the characters react to those words. Did the exchange move the story forward? Did it change the relationship between the characters? Sometimes, dialogue can summarize actions up to this point in the story, with conflict over what actions need to come next. This elevation of tension and conflict is exactly what needs to be created repeatedly.

Takeaway One: Dialogue can provide important information in a much more interesting manner for the reader. When a reader is an eyewitness to a conversation, it is action, rather than telling.

Takeaway Two: Dialogue keeps the story moving while adding a distinct voice and characterization to your characters. No two people speak the same way, and neither should your characters.

Takeaway Three: Learn to use dialect or vernacular in dialogue. These things can breathe life into your story, but too much can distract and annoy the reader.

Takeaway Four: Character reactions can enhance the significance of dialogue.

17

QUICK CHECKLIST FOR SUCCESS

"This writing business. Pencils and whatnot. Overrated, if you ask me. Silly stuff. Nothing to it."

—*Eeyore, in Winnie the Pooh (1926) Chapter 10, by A.A. Milne*

"A lot of people think writers wake up in the middle of the night with inspiration, but it's better to get a good night's sleep because you'll have a hard day of work tomorrow."

—*Shelby Foote*

Use this checklist of ingredients to verify you have all the magic spells necessary to make your work sparkle and shine. These key aspects will bewitch contest judges and readers alike. And, as we've already seen, placing a sparkle in a judge's eye can lead to an agent agreement or a publishing contract.

Setting

☐ Verify you have given your reader a sense of place. (Chapter

Nine) Unless told otherwise, readers will assume your work is in the present, in the world we know. If you deviate from this standard, let your reader know by providing setting information, such as: "Jupiter, earth date 5439" or "Scottish Highlands, 1302."

☐ Ensure your setting transmits a unified feel to your readers. Think about the film *The Wizard of Oz*. The black and white Kansas farm and the colorful Land of Oz settings are as important to the heart of the story as the main characters.

Action

☐ Your story starts with action. Dusty Richards once said, "If you can't bring yourself to the action of your story without writing yourself there, then write yourself there. After you do that, cut out all the words before the action. Put the words in a safe place, because you might use them later. But most likely, you'll see the actual story starts with the action."

☐ You seasoned your work with history but avoided flashbacks and backstory and kept the action moving forward.

☐ You used short, curt sentences in action scenes.

☐ You added physical reactions, such as sweaty palms, racing heart, or feeling weak in the legs.

Characters

☐ Your characters are well-drawn but not over-described, allowing the reader to fill in features and personality. Example: "He was as lean as a whippet, with eyes that pierced to the truth."

A law enforcement background deprived him of a sense of humor."

☐ Your characters are not all the same. They have quirks that show how they fit into their world. These quirks can be as simple as how they walk or push through a crowd, what they do when forced to remain seated for a long time, how they lose themselves in their phones.

Passion

It's easy to pull readers into a story if you're passionate about your subject. *Uncle Tom's Cabin* is a book that helped launch a war and changed the lives of many people. The author, Harriet Beecher Stowe, was passionate about ending slavery. Her passion, shared through her writing, put a human face on the evils of slavery.

☐ You creatively dropped in tidbits of history or realism to keep your readers invigorated in the storyline.

☐ Your characters don't spray too many facts in their dialogue. Dialogue is a great way to drop in these pieces. A morsel here or there usually works, but only that.

Point of view

☐ Confirm you have chosen the best point of view (Chapter 12). Nonfiction is told in the technical first-person point of view, which means an author-narrator is doing the telling. In fiction, you decide which point of view best shows your story. In a novel, one point of view per scene is a simple transition for most readers.

Literary (poetic) devices

☐ You have employed literary devices and imagery to heighten your reader's emotional experience through tools such as alliteration, rhyme, simile, and metaphor. (Chapter 15). Using literary imagery appeals to a reader's senses and creates an image or idea in their head. It evokes a creative response in the reader and expands the description through this creative response. Used sparingly, a light fairy dusting of literary devices makes your work shine.

Memorable endings

☐ You resolved all important outstanding issues. No need to tell us or show us everything. What is unwritten but implied makes a powerful ending.

☐ Your ending rings true, avoids cliches or tricks, and is honest. A famous ending that warms our hearts is the last line of *A Christmas Carol* by Charles Dickens. At the end, we wonder whether Scrooge will do enough to keep Tiny Tim from dying. The narrative tells us Tiny Tim doesn't die and Scrooge becomes a second father to him. The last line is, "And so, as Tiny Tim observed, 'God Bless Us Every One!'" Readers are left with the comfort of a happy ending but allowed to decide for themselves the details beyond the close of the story.

☐ If you include a surprise or twist ending, it is unexpected but within the realm of possibility for your story world.

For your writing to win contests, win over agents or publishers, or win readers, the real magic potion is hard work. Learn everything you can about the craft. Then keep writing and dreaming, because one day your dream will come true.

Takeaway One: Immediately give your readers a sense of place.

Takeaway Two: Start your story with action. It hooks the reader to become engaged in your story.

Takeaway Three: Write about a subject you are passionate about. Your passion transfers to your work in powerful ways.

Takeaway Four: Choose the best point of view to tell your story.

Takeaway Five: Sprinkle the fairy dust of literary devices into your work, such as imagery and humor.

Takeaway Six: Create a memorable ending.

18

EMBRACING THE RED PEN

"Just know that everyone's writing is terrible. Until it's not. You gotta work it. Refine it. Shape it. Spend time with it. It's a relationship. Not easy. Gonna be terrible before it's not. And that's okay."

—*Ava DuVernay, filmmaker and screenwriter*

"If it sounds like writing, I rewrite it."

—*Elmore Leonard*

When you've completed your first draft, celebrate. Congratulations! Many writers give up before they type "The End." Now comes the time to edit your work. Wave that red pen like a magic wand and make your errors vanish.

Writers need times of solitude to become a success. Editing greatness takes place in the confinement of your lonely writer's studio. Yes, you can and should participate in critique groups, but when it comes down to the actual first editing pass, only you can decide, typically in seclusion, whether the input of others adds to your story or detracts. Kurt Vonnegut once said, "Start your story as close as possible to the end." Most people can't do this in the writing process but can trim it in the editing process.

After writing your piece, editing is the single most important step in the writing process. It's been said many times that "editing is putting every word on trial for its life," found in *Reading Like a Writer* by Francine Prose. Let me clarify: This round of editing is not the same as securing a professional edit. (See more on this in Chapter 19.) This round is you cleaning up your story, deepening it, and revealing it fully.

When you've completed several rounds of this kind of editing, you may question why so much analysis goes into something that is an art. The craft of writing is difficult. When you've edited your work properly, you've removed not only the bad, but also the mediocre from your pages. All that remains is the pure magic. Your readers will treasure these enchanted pages.

Editing has many iterations.

- **Line editing** is sometimes called copy editing, but there is a difference. A copy edit's purpose is to correct grammar, punctuation, and spelling. A line edit literally goes "line by line," considering word choice, fact-checking, flow, pacing, sentence length, and more. A copy edit can be done simultaneously with a line edit.
- **Content editing**, sometimes referred to as developmental editing, involves character development and large-scale issues such as the flow of the story, the plotting, and the "threads" or arc of the story.
- **Proofreading** is a whole other kind of wizardry. Proofreaders find errors missed by editing and other reviewers. They check minute details and such formatting issues as indentations, typeface, and page number sequences.

Magic Words

As a writer, you must do all the editing described above. Although you may think editing a short story or poetry is easy, it's not. It's my practice to address one issue each time I read through my piece. I'm also a big believer in allowing enough time (days or even weeks) to pass from one review to another to help catch what needs to be changed.

Beta readers can help, but you will still need to do the work of cleaning up what they find. A beta reader is not a relative but is someone who will be brutally honest without being mean. Always ask your beta readers (yes, you may well have more than one) to mark the page where they stopped reading to do something else. If all of your beta readers stop in the same place, this tells you your action declines there. This is something to fix before submitting to contests.

Example: Say you begin with, "A man in a hat walked into the room." With editing, it becomes, "The man in a black coat pushes his way past the receptionist and insists he must speak to a detective." Descriptions should go from broad to specific when you edit. This helps clarify the story and adds richness.

Consider editing your character's name. A character's name is important and can tell a reader so much about them. Scarlett O'Hara was initially named Pansy. Margaret Mitchell changed it to Scarlett, as it was a stronger name for a strong character.

J. K. Rowling, author of the Harry Potter books, is one of the best with creative character names. She researched names from literature, mythology, history, as well as graveyards and phone books. The alliteration of Severus Snape is genius, yet she also chose Severus because it translates to severe.

Edit your descriptions to keep them short and sweet, plus make your words show character. A man can say, "I don't have a lot of money," or "I swear I'll never be poor again." The second example is much more revealing.

Some people write the specific details from the beginning. Others start with something general, like their character is in a construction yard, then edit, such as, "he jumped off the bulldozer and twisted his ankle. As he limped away, his cell phone rang. He dropped it when he pulled it from his pocket."

Editing mishaps: Confessions from the guilty

All of us want to be perfect writers. However, the qualifications for being a perfect writer appear too steep for me to master. Do I write a perfect tale? No. Do I edit my work with perfection? Sadly, again, the answer is no.

Here is a better way to evaluate my work—and your work, as well: Do I write my tale as perfectly as my current skills allow me to? Yes. Do I try to do the best editing I can muster? Yes. My best effort still lacks perfection, so I strive to improve in all areas by learning from my mistakes and learning from other writers and editors. I wish I made no editing mistakes, but I'm guilty of a few. Unfortunately, my humanity and my complicated life stand in the way of perfection.

But here's what I do, and what you can aim for. I work toward perfection, and I double-check my actions to ensure they are correct. But, sometimes, I still miss something—and you will too.

It's somewhat comparable to clicking your car remote more times than necessary. The act of double- and triple-clicking reassures you that you've locked the car. But does repeated locking result in your car being "more locked"? It's a way to check yourself, but it may not solve the issue. An extra set of eyes that belong to an editor or a fellow author might get you that extra "lockiness" you desire.

In two recent contests, I entered a story, the same story, and failed to catch a mistake. Even after multiple edits. What was the mistake? I'd inadvertently changed the name of one of my minor characters toward the end of the story. Not once did I notice Patience had turned into Prudence.

Learning about the mistake filled me with horror. The sheer number of times I'd edited the piece should have caught this error. I'm sincerely grateful to the contest judge who mentioned it. Sadly, it was after I'd sent the entry off to the second contest, but I found and killed that editing mistake for any future use of the story.

How do these things happen? That particular mistake occurred because I'd deliberated between two similar character names. After completing my editing on the story several times, I failed to notice the name I ended with was *not* the name I started with for this character.

All I can do now—and all you can do when it happens to you—is learn from the mistake. I am grateful for the judge who pointed it out so I could fix it. I do not know how long I would have been "blind" to the error, and it could have haunted the piece for a much longer time. Perhaps I would have spotted it if I'd read the story aloud more than once. Reading your work aloud allows your ears to help you edit things your eyes may pass over.

If you're lucky enough to have someone willing to read your contest entries, take advantage of that gift. Fresh eyes, advising you about things they might notice, are priceless. They don't have to be professional grammarians. They need to be someone who will pay attention to your story and advise of anything they noticed, didn't understand, or "tripped over" while they were reading. Feedback from someone who hasn't had your story whispering around in their head for weeks and months is a treasure.

As much as we would like to be perfect writers, we are not. Just do your best and learn from your mistakes. In this example, I learned never to consider two similar character names. In the future, I will contemplate different names, so any mistaken substitution is a jarring, obvious error to spot. I hope. Another tip is, if you decide to change a character's name, do a search of the document for the original name and replace any overlooked corrections with the correct name.

Above all, learn to forgive yourself for any mistake that slips under the radar. Writing is a passion, a craft, and an art. We learn from everything we do. I salute you for choosing this art form. Do your best but forgive yourself if your work is not perfect. Move on to the next contest entry.

Items to remove or improve during editing

Check the guidelines of the contest or publisher where you plan to submit your work. You must format your manuscript exactly as they request. Formatting guidelines are obligatory, not optional. They may disqualify your work before even reading it if you don't follow their rules. Most require Times New Roman font, 12-point, double-spaced, with a 0.5" first-line indent. Verify what they want and then provide that.

Analyze your work for passive voice and replace the phrasing with active voice as much as possible. An easy way to eliminate passive voice is to start the sentence with the subject, then add the verb and the object. Passive voice happens when the sentence structure is reversed, such as starting with the object, then the verb, and then the subject. Sometimes, passive voice is necessary for your work. Eliminate all passive-voice sentences except those that are necessary.

Hunt down your adjectives and adverbs and eliminate as many as possible. Mark Twain and Stephen King have gone on record about these little troublemakers, and they know how to write well. Adding them slows the pace of your work, while removing them will strengthen and quicken your work.

Analyze your work for repetitions. It's fine to describe your main character as tall. After that, emphasize "tall" without repeating the word. For example, substitute "She gazed toward the window, glancing over the heads of most people in the room."

Seek and destroy any repetitious words. With mysteries, I tend to overuse the words investigation or information. Do a word search and find a synonym that works. I also am guilty of using short descriptors too frequently, such as "He nodded." or "She smiled."

A nickname for a character distracted me in one book where the author used it too many times. I wanted to throw the book against the wall because the repetition drove me crazy. These things take a reader out of the story. I was also irritated because the repeated nickname downgraded a good story.

Allow yourself plenty of time to edit when approaching a deadline. Until I'm mired in the middle of editing, I forget, or cannot appreciate, how much time it takes for each step of the editing process. Give yourself the time to search for each editing item. Your work will shine because of it.

Analyze your work for telling versus showing. You want to show your readers a story, not tell them a story. In my first draft, I purposely implement telling to get the story or chapter written in digital form. With my second and later drafts, I look for places of "telling" and turn them into conversations, arguments, or other active forms of showing. The initial draft is a sprint with ideas. Subsequent drafts are marathons necessary to improve the ideas by turning them into action.

Review your work for conflict. It can be internal or external, but a story is lackluster if there is no conflict or tension.

Head hopping is a terrible sickness, but we can cure it. Stick to one point of view in each scene. Sometimes it's hard to identify when you've changed the point of view. I'm still working on mastering that skill.

Know the grammar mistakes you most often make. One of my ongoing weaknesses is misplaced modifiers. Using weak verbs instead of active verbs is also curable. Substitute "sauntered" or "ambled" instead of "walked" for a character who is catlike or animated. Replacing "talked" with "chatted" or "gossiped" breathes more life into the character.

Less is more. I'm a chatty person, and my writing reflects the same proclivity. I learned years ago that removing words improves your story. It happened when I had a 2,500-word story that was perfect for a contest, except the contest limit was 2,000 words. I didn't reduce the words all at once. I set a goal to remove one hundred words per review. When I'd whittled down the five hundred words, I didn't even miss them, and the story was intrinsically better.

Look for "gawking" characters and remove the phrases that signal the "gawking." We create these when we, as authors, force our way into the story between the action and the reader. An example is, "I saw Bobby Ray at the drugstore" vs. "Bobby Ray was at the drugstore." Review for "She watched," "He heard," and other related phrases that signal you've written in a passive, intrusive way. Remove them. Look for "gawking" in dialogue and your general prose.

Write in the "positive" for ease of reader understanding. It can reduce your word count and clarify the point you're trying to make. Examples: "He didn't want anyone to bother him." (Negative) "He wanted to be alone." (Positive) "It wouldn't be long before the sun would set." (Negative) "The sun will set soon," or "Soon, the moon will rise." (Positive)

The path to contest wins is paved with powerful language

By using the strongest language possible in your contest entry, you'll mesmerize your judges and earn your way to contest awards. During your editing process, identify any weak words and phrases you've used and remove them. Substitute a strong word for your initial weak choice or obliterate the weak word or phrase.

The word "very" can be used as an adverb (to a high standard or degree), such as "very happy," or as an adjective (actual or precise), "This is the very car my father owned." Do a word search for any "very" used in your piece and substitute a better word, if you need one. For example, instead of very sad, consider despondent. Instead of very happy, employ ecstatic. Words such as despondent or ecstatic are richer and convey more meaning. Instead of "the very car my father owned," the phrase "the exact car" appears stronger.

Some weak modifiers are "rather," "quite," "somehow," "somewhat," and similar adverbs. You do not have to get rid of all of them. Review your work and see how many you have in your story. Consider whether you need a substitute word or phrase for most of them. I like to sprinkle a few of these adverb types in dialogue to make it sound more lifelike.

The word "that" is a four-letter word. There are many ways to use it—and it can almost always be removed. It can be a pronoun, as in "That is her house." Or, a determiner, such as "Look at that dog." It can be an adverb, "Well, I wouldn't take his argument that far." And, as a conjunction in several ways. One way is to express a reason, such as "It thrilled Mom that I came home." When used as a conjunction, the word "that" can be eliminated for easier reading without the loss of any meaning. For example, "It thrilled Mom I came home," doesn't need "that." (Better still: "My return home thrilled Mom," which avoids using the pronoun "it" without an antecedent.) It's your call while editing, but most times, the loss of "that" strengthens a sentence.

Use Microsoft Word's search and replace tool to find all uses of "get" (present tense) and "got" (past tense or past participle). Then, replace them with active, solid verbs. There are so many stronger verbs to choose from and here are a few to consider: receive, earn, win, obtain, come by, acquire, appropriate, and procure.

We each have our favorite words or phrases. Figure out what yours are, and then check to ensure you don't overuse them. For example, the word "such" can be used as a determiner, predeterminer, and a pronoun. It can slip into your work like a ninja. "Such a mess!" "Any old such thing is okay with me." While editing, replace these old favorites with stronger language.

Read your work aloud. Although I've repeatedly suggested this, this editing aid cannot be stressed too much. Listening to the rhythm of your sentences will identify unnecessary or weak words.

Never throw away a storyline, chapter, or plot point. Put what you've written in a file folder specifically for possible reuse or redesigning. Review that folder frequently to see if you can resurrect your discarded words. You might find you love something you've previously rejected just as it is. Or make a copy and start changing things. It's amazing how many nuggets of good ideas get buried beneath poor plotlines.

This applies to chapters from novels. When writing a series, if you don't like a chapter, put it in a reject folder that moves to the next book in the series. It might fit better in a later storyline, or the passage of time may reward you with better skills to handle that plot line.

Chapter 19 will address using a professional editor. Although they cost money, it can be money well spent. A professional can teach you editing issues you didn't know you didn't know. They can also elevate your work to a contest-winning level. This is something to consider with your manuscript or contest entries of higher regard.

Takeaway One: After writing your piece, editing is the single most important step in the writing process.

Takeaway Two: Establish a list of items to review when you begin editing. The more you edit, the more you learn to remove or leave out while you are drafting, making editing easier.

Takeaway Three: Identify weak words and phrases you've used and remove them. Substitute a strong word for your initial weak choice or obliterate the weak word or phrase.

19

PROFESSIONAL EDITING

"The difference between the 'almost right' word and the 'right' word is really a large matter ... 'tis the difference between the lightning bug and the lightning."

—*Mark Twain*

Writing is difficult. Editing your work is necessary and beneficial, as we saw in the previous chapter. If you have the means and the inclination to hire a professional to help you with the editing process, do it. This decision can take your work product from acceptable to contest winner.

When you're trying to catch the attention of an agent or a publisher, it is well worth the money to have a professional editor apply their talents to your work. The ultimate goal is to impress the agent or publisher, and mistakes, whether in grammar or content, will not give them the right impression.

Once you have a publisher, they will provide editors to you at no cost. Celebrate your good fortune, review every suggestion they make, and learn to be flexible where you can. Standing your ground for a particular issue may be necessary, but be malleable.

Your publisher and editor or editors will appreciate that you are "coachable" and willing to learn from those in the know.

Do individuals without an agent or a publisher need a professional editor? The goal of editing is to remove all the bad, unnecessary, or mediocre words and thoughts from your pages. In theory, this means you'll be left with only the good stuff. Your personal involvement in writing every word may lead to bias in determining what is considered "good." This is where the input of a professional can improve and elevate your work.

Whether you are self-publishing, entering a contest, or submitting your manuscript for traditional publication, hiring a professional can make a significant difference in the quality of your work. If you enter competitive contests with short fiction or self-publish your manuscript, the cost of a professional editor is money well spent. Don't lose readers because of typos and plot holes that could have been fixed if you'd only known about them.

Are you a highly skilled grammarian? Then you may check your grammar, punctuation, and spelling. If you're not the best at grammar, you can learn an incredible amount from a professional Line Editor/Copy Editor. I'm not the best grammarian, and learned from all the suggestions made by my line editor. The point is to have an expert apply their skills to your work.

Is the plot for your novel perfect in layout, story arc, and flow? Content, or developmental, editing, involves character development. It also includes large-scale issues like the flow of the story, plotting, and the "threads" or arc of the story.

A content editor notes continuity issues. An example would be your failure to "set up" a change of clothes for a character or a change in the name of a character within the manuscript. They are the ones who catch when a bottle that falls off a table hadn't been mentioned until it crashed on the floor. Another example is "head hopping" as it relates to point of view. Can you identify these things, along with all the other items in an edit, and fix them?

Another type of sorcerer, called a proofreader, finds errors missed by editors and reviewers. They double-check all the minute details.

Some professional editors can do all the editing, in phases. Other professionals specialize in specific skills. Research what you need and want. Ask for references from your top picks and contact their references for a detailed evaluation.

Any editor must be careful not to edit out your author's voice.

Publishers and agents can have acquisition editors who know what the publisher or agent requires. It is their job to review submissions to determine if the submission and the author meet the requirements of the publishing house or agent. They also screen submissions to ensure the writer is coachable and teachable.

I've had good and bad experiences with professional editors. In the not-so-good experience, I asked for recommendations from a fellow writer. I contacted several professional editors about the job. Only one of those contacted could do everything that needed to be done on the project. While the editor did a fine job of suggesting corrections, formatting the book for printing, and working on a timeline, she did not have a pleasant personality. Most of her communication was by email, at her choice, and it appeared she hadn't read what I sent her. The experience was not a happy one for me. I completed the project, but I was leery of doing anything like that again.

When I was blessed with a publishing contract, the editors performed two types of edits on my first manuscript. A content edit and then a line edit, done by different people. My experience with both of them differed completely from the editor of the other project. I learned so much and enjoyed the process.

Since then, I've had several books edited, and it was the same positive experience. I'm grateful for the opportunity to learn from these editors and improve my skills.

Editors can save you from yourself. I wrote a scene where there was a two-floor drop of a character onto a soft-landing area, but the drop would have been over thirty feet. An editor nixed this as unrealistic. The editor believed readers would feel such a drop could hurt the character. I shortened the drop to one story. After publishing, readers have never commented on the height of the drop. That is exactly the correction my story needed, but I was too close to it to "let it happen" without the suggestion of the editor.

Takeaway One: For important manuscript submissions, self-publishing, and highly regarded contests, consider hiring a professional editor.

Takeaway Two: Professional editing should allow your work to impress an agent or publisher. Mistakes you don't catch, whether grammar or content, will not give them a favorable impression.

Takeaway Three: If you have the opportunity to work with professional editors, take it. Learn from them and improve your skills.

20

NONFICTION WRITING

"An autobiography usually reveals nothing bad about its writer except his memory."

—*Franklin P. Jones*

Earlier, I wrote that my path to publication came in three key ways. First, by gaining an education at writer's conferences. Second, through participating in writing groups. Third, through experience writing for newspapers and magazines. Some of you may take the same path I did to achieve your publication success.

Fiction and nonfiction writers will find much of the shared information helpful. But in this chapter, I want to share some tips and tricks for nonfiction writers. It may well be that you fiction folk will also find gems worth excavating here.

A tremendous resource for the paying market for writers, including playwrights and screenwriting, is the periodical publication, *Writer's Market*, published annually by Penguin Random House. The sister publications, *Guide to Literary Agents*, *Children's Writer's & Illustrator's Market*, *Novel & Short Story*

Writer's Market, and *Poet's Market,* are industry-standard resources for contest information, awards, agents, and much more. Many libraries will carry these annually, and you'll find them in the reference section.

Opportunities abound for writers in the nonfiction arena. Learn the specifics you need to submit to these markets by researching each entity's submission guidelines and following them to the letter. Some will prefer a short email contact, while others will prefer a one-page query letter or even the completed article for consideration. Many of them are paying markets.

Below is an overview of the types of nonfiction writing.

Essays

Most essays are a snapshot—a slice of pie, not the whole pie. They are written about your one point and are best if kept to one, possibly two, scenes. Make the topic something close to your heart; a personal experience, personal observation, told in the way you see things. What may seem unimportant to you now could be important to others in the future.

Inspirational writing has the purpose of uplifting. The writer wants to produce or arouse a feeling or thought. You're hoping to shine a light into the darkness a potential reader is experiencing. To make the world a better place. To pull a reader up from feeling powerless or hopeless.

The category includes devotionals (specifically spiritual writing) as well as works that motivate and move people. Examples of these include Harriet Beecher Stowe's *Uncle Tom's Cabin,* which humanized slavery and inflamed a civil war. Other examples: Abraham Lincoln's Gettysburg Address; John F. Kennedy's "Ask not what your country can do for you, ask what you can do for your country" speech; and Dr. Martin Luther King's "I Have a Dream" speech. Each was a collection of written words before the orators inflamed them for the ages with their impassioned deliveries, quoted beyond anyone's imagination.

Inspirational writing is also shorter. You can inspire someone through a note in a lunchbox. This is providing inspiration for someone without being paid or published. Your reward is to make that person feel better or encouraged. It's still motivational and inspirational writing.

Even that's not all, however. An article in a magazine or newspaper similar to "How to drop twenty pounds in forty days" is inspirational or motivational writing. Published collections of essays, such as *Chicken Soup for the Soul* and *Cup of Comfort*, are extremely popular and invite writers to submit their work. They publish essays that are not preachy but give people hope to overcome a problem or understand what's happening in their lives. These collections do offer payment to authors who are selected, as well as the all-important publishing credits.

Journalism

There are various style guides, sometimes called manuals, related to journalism. (Review Chapter 12.) It is important to note that styles will vary from publication to publication among newspapers and other print journalism. They have their own "in-house" style, even though their "in-house" guides are typically strongly linked to certain style manuals, such as AP style or Chicago Manual of Style. When researching submission guidelines, be aware of the style manual or guide recommended by that publication.

Newspapers: Writing the news requires an ability to identify the main points of the story and weave them into the shortest, most direct retelling of them while keeping the article interesting. The space allotted for a newspaper article, whether in print or online, is small because space is money. Newspapers, especially dailies, are constantly under deadline. There is no time to "flop about" with technical issues related to writing. A news writer must keep their words direct, compelling, and accurate while honing their language and grammar skills to a keen edge. Taking scientific or technical information and transforming it into concepts the public can understand is a skill and an art.

A wonderful guide to learning how to write for newspapers is *The Associated Press Guide to News Writing*, Fourth Edition, by Rene J. Cappon.

Magazines: Writing for magazines usually requires publication experience or an editor with a keen eye for spotting talent that can be quickly developed. You can suggest a topic for their repeating columns and articles, or you can pitch an article idea. Many times, this is done with a query letter.

Query letters are your opportunity to pitch your article idea and must also reference your previous writing experience. Treat recipients with respect and make each query representative of your best writing. I recommend *Writer's Digest Handbook of Magazine Article Writing* as your first stop in reference material related to writing for magazines.

I earned publication experience writing for a local residential community magazine. That gig led to publication in regional magazines, which led to a national magazine, and eventually an international magazine. Even though I am a published fiction author, I still write for the local residential community magazine and an electronic writer's magazine. Don't snub your nose at local publications. It is reliable work and keeps your nonfiction skills current.

Literary magazines typically publish short stories, poetry, and essays. Some feature book reviews, author profiles and interviews, as well as literary criticism.

Periodicals for specific audiences are referred to as trade publications. Examples include *Science Monthly*, *Farmer's Almanac*, and *ACHRNews*—a weekly magazine for contractors focusing on residential and commercial heating, ventilation, air conditioning, and refrigeration installation and service. Most major industries have at least one trade publication.

Nonfiction books

Books that are true in content, not fictional or fantasy, are nonfiction. They are based on facts, actual events, and real people, such as biographies or historical works. Writing this nonfiction book is rewarding for me. Knowing I am providing a tool to help others pursue a dream or a goal is inspiring. My goal is to encourage writers like you and provide some shortcuts to how the goal of winning contests and getting published can be accomplished.

> **Autobiography:** an account of a person's life written by that person. Generally, it's an entire life story, told chronologically.
>
> **Biography.** A factual account about another person written about a historical or famous figure.
>
> **Memoir:** a historical account or biography written from a personal perspective or a special source or learned subject.
>
> **Creative nonfiction:** This category includes memoirs, personal essays, articles, and some books. Writers of creative nonfiction take an event and apply creative writing techniques to immerse the reader into the scene. Works can be an "embellishment" to the facts, but creative nonfiction should remain as accurate as possible to remain a nonfiction work.

For example, we don't remember the exact words our parents might have used in a situation when we flushed something down the toilet and it overflowed the bowl. However, we remember their emotions related to the situation and cleanup. As an adult recalling such an event, you might look back at it with humor or use it as a teaching tool for young children. However, when it occurred, I doubt you found anything humorous about the reaction your parents exhibited and any punishment they gave.

Linda Apple, in her book, *Writing Life: Your Story Matters!* said, "Using creative nonfiction is like painting pictures and portraits with words." Writing craft techniques used in creative nonfiction include almost everything available in fiction, such as dialogue, emotions, sensory descriptions, and observations.

Documenting stories about family members and family gatherings is important work. You're writing the history for a future generation. Sometimes, the gift of a family story at Christmastime can be more precious than an expensive present.

Takeaway One: Nonfiction experience may result in a successful career in both nonfiction and fiction writing. Writing experience of any kind is good to have. My nonfiction experience helped me understand another side of the publishing business.

Takeaway Two: Experience is worth a lot of money. Being paid for your work is imperative, but you may need to gather experience and publication clippings through volunteer work to get your foot in the publication door. Your time is valuable, but experience is something you may need to gather at your own cost initially until you can approach entities for pay.

Takeaway Three: Start with small publications and work your way to larger or more expansive periodicals. Or build an excellent reputation and stay with a publication that appreciates your work. Either way, it shows agents and publishers you are a capable writer.

Takeaway Four: Documenting stories about family members and family gatherings is important writer's work. You're producing a written history for future generations.

21

BELIEVING IN THE MAGIC

"I never dreamed about success. I worked for it."

—Estee' Lauder

"If you believe in the impossible, and work tirelessly to achieve it, you can create your own magic, your own luck, and your own possibilities."

—Journalist Kate Sullivan, describing David Copperfield

Writing is hard work. Bouncing back after multiple rejections associated with your writing is even harder. Those who succeed at writing never give up. They keep writing until they learn enough skills and techniques that they get noticed. Successful writers have grit. It's the quality that won't allow them to quit when things are tough.

Victor Hugo wrote in the nude, so he wouldn't leave his desk. Betty Smith, author of *A Tree Grows in Brooklyn*, said she never *found* the time to write. She had to *make* the time to write. Teach yourself how to write and take notes about your writing in places where you have time to kill. You can write ideas or craft scenes while waiting in the reception area of your doctor's office. If a creative idea hits while driving, record a voice memo on your phone and type it up later.

Feeding your creativity

When I say to myself, "Today, you must produce some terrific writing," it rarely happens. My creative spark or muse needs to be fed a constant diet of artistic inspiration—not just coerced at the last minute. Is it a magic potion? Not really. Here are some ideas for you. Not all will work for everyone, but one or two of these things will likely resonate with you.

Always be ready for sudden and unexpected ideas. Those initial sparks of thought are extremely important to preserve. This is when I use the notes feature on my phone or search for paper and pen. The act of writing it down or preserving it in digital form is important. You think the idea is so good you couldn't possibly forget it. I can't tell you how many times I had to learn that was not an accurate thought. Write it down or record the idea.

One of my favorite scenes in a movie related to the creative spark of writing is in the movie *Finding Jane*. Jane Austen, played by Anne Hathaway, walks away from a group in conversation to write a sudden thought or inspiration. I laughed out loud when I saw it because, 1) it's a writer joke, and 2) writers do this.

Allow time for that initial idea to simmer. Most of us need this phase to examine, debate, consider, explain, and possibly outline the initial idea. I call it ruminating, pondering, or cogitating. It's the time you need to wrestle with an idea before you write anything.

Don't rush the process. Let it roll around in your head like a pinball until you've refined the idea enough to do more with it. Don't ruminate in front of your laptop. Take a walk in your neighborhood. Be inspired by beautiful art by touring an art gallery or attending a play or musical. When traveling, enjoy an audiobook or your favorite tunes while you cogitate your story options. I've had brilliant ideas hit me when I'm doing something routine, like vacuuming, washing clothes, or driving.

We have grown used to instant gratification. We're often impatient with things that need time to mature. But you, as a writer, need time to nurture the idea and decide the best way it can work for you. Is it a poem? Play? Short story? Draft a few sentences of a poem or lines of dialogue and see where it goes. You don't have to pen *War and Peace*; just try a paragraph of thought to see where the idea might take you. Don't forget to experiment with an unusual ending or phrase. It might be the zest needed to win a contest.

Refresh and reset

In the many hours I spend writing each week, few reward me with the experience I call "writing Zen." I define "writing Zen" as a laser focus on my work, with magic pouring out of my typing fingers. The suggestions below don't apply when you're experiencing those rare but magnificent writing periods.

Instead, these hints are for the times when you struggle to get your point across. Or when you've reached a crossroads, with no clear path forward for your story or characters. I hope my experience will help you if you find yourself in the same predicament.

We all get frustrated with our writing. My frustration always seems to happen when I'm staring down a deadline—and I'm blinking. Whether it's a publishing deadline or a contest deadline, they can be ugly when your writing is not where you want it to be. I tell myself, "I only need an epiphany, just one epiphany, to reach the deadline and submit my piece."

So, what do I do?

I abandon my mission and step away. Step away from a deadline? Yep. The act of stepping away from my workspace is a rebellious move, but one that has paid off for me many times. Performing a quick chore or going for a brisk walk can help settle the blowing sandstorm of my creativity.

Stepping away, leaving your words behind, can be a magical act akin to the power of the amazing magician, David Copperfield. When I'm forcing my brain to be creative, it sometimes rebels. Walking away and doing something routine, like running a load of clothes in the washer or taking a shower, frees my creative chains. While I'm engaged in a routine act, often something I can do just through muscle memory, the solution to my dilemma presents itself.

Persistence and prioritizing

Every writer on the planet could do something else instead of writing. Successful writers are persistent, and they make writing a priority. To find success, we must embrace persistence in our writing. We must firmly (or perhaps pigheadedly) pursue the writing craft, despite difficulty or opposition.

Over the years, out of all the issues associated with the writing craft, I've struggled the most with making my writing a priority. That's one reason I love contests and those beautiful things called contest deadlines.

Initially, I didn't appreciate the beauty of a contest deadline. It took years before I embraced them as the gift they are. The ugly experiences of missing deadlines opened my eyes to how necessary it is to organize my time. If I wanted to be a writer—and I did—I had to carve out more time to write and plan with lists and notes about contest entry ideas, long before there was an impending deadline.

It took some effort to set boundaries for the importance of my writing. It's easy to say, "I'll write tomorrow if you need me to do X today." When I was working full time, I didn't have any creative energy left after working a full-time job, evening meal preparation, and cleaning up. Saturday mornings and Sunday afternoons were my writing time. I found *my* consistency in setting time for my writing caused my family to also respect those boundaries.

I used to spend half a day "getting this done" and "getting that done" before I allowed myself to sit down and write. Whether it was laundry, cleaning, or some other chore that needed doing, writing took a back seat to it. But then those beautiful deadlines loomed. Those lovely, beautiful deadlines. If I want to submit to a contest with a deadline and that deadline is fast approaching, then I can justify putting my writing ahead of something else "that needs to be done," because I'm on a time limitation here.

Retirement from my first career has allowed me to spend much more time with my writing as a priority. Even with extra time devoted to writing, I can't sit and write for hours on end. I've discovered I work best if I write for an hour or two, then step away and perform a chore or action. The amazing thing is my writing comes with me inside my head while I complete the assignment. Many times, I've raced back to my desk to scribble a note about this character thought or that plot twist and then returned to my duties.

Once I return to my writing table again, I'm glad to be there. My hastily scribbled note is waiting for me, like the inspiration it is. It's a reward for persistence and prioritizing. I hope all of you find it in your writing.

The beginning of success

I will never forget the first time my name was called for an award in a writing contest. It was for Third Honorable Mention. Some writers might snarl at that placement, but it meant the world to me. It still does. That wonderful Third Honorable Mention was more than my first writing award—it provided proof that two years of hard work and study had improved my writing from having never placed in a contest to number six of the top six entries.

Some judges of contests won't award any honorable mentions unless an entry is exemplary. For judges with this mindset, please reconsider. Awards are for exemplary work. But they are also a lifeline for writers who strive for excellence and have reached the cusp of it. That honorable mention I received was hope, handed to me by a proud writer's conference volunteer. It allowed me to believe in myself, my skills, and my work.

But remember, our work will not appeal to all judges. However, *our* belief in our talent and ability is the first step forward with our dreams of writing. Each step of learning and adapting better methods is part of every writer's journey.

Another gift in the world of creative writing is the friends and colleagues you come to know at seminars, conferences, and through writing groups. Who doesn't enjoy friends who understand your creativity and determination to improve your writing? The ability to share our thoughts, ideas, style of writing, and goals with other writers should be cherished.

I've encountered new writers who are concerned about plagiarism if they share their work with a writing group or a mentor. Real writers don't want your work, they have plenty of ideas of their own. Real writers want to help you elevate your work. Even though we may compete in various contests, most writers are thrilled when their friends garner awards. They help and encourage each other without jealousy. Many times, when your friends climb the ladder of success, they can then reach down and give you a hand to help you climb with them.

Be open to learning. Writing is not an easy vocation, but it is rewarding if you muscle through the hard parts and appreciate the joy. Grit and determination make successful writers. Author Richard Bach said, "As a writer, the biggest talent you can have is determination."

Remember: Believe in the magic of words. The idea of

magic, in this sense, is hopeful. It's something like a reward or a gift beyond our usual grasp that's intriguing. You bring the magic to the words. That means *you* are the magic. Work hard, believe in yourself, and make the magic happen.

Takeaway One: Be receptive when a sudden and unexpected idea comes to you. That initial spark of thought is important to preserve. Write it down and ponder it.

Takeaway Two: Make writing a priority. Successful writers are persistent and carve out time for writing. It doesn't have to be every day, but a consistent schedule for writing is a "must do" item on your "to-do" list.

Takeaway Three: Accept that learning, studying the craft, and being open to suggestions are vital to achieving your writing goals.

Takeaway Four: *You* are the magic. Believe in yourself and your abilities.

GLOSSARY OF TERMS

Action: Occurs when something happens that makes or permits something else to happen.

Acquisitions editor: An editor who evaluates manuscripts for a publisher or agent. Some negotiate contracts for the publisher and aid in the production of the book.

Agent: A person who acts on behalf of another person or group. With authors, an agent represents the interest of the author with publishers.

Antihero: A main character that cannot have heroic qualities.

Aside: An interruption of your dominant story to communicate an event or events prior to the current scene.

Backstory: History or background of a fictional character.

Beta reader: A proofreader (not a relative) who will be brutally honest without being mean. Another writer or grammarian can help you with grammar issues, typos, and content questions.

Glossary of Terms

Book influencers: People who share their favorite reads with others, usually through social media.

Characterization: The artistic representation of a fictional character.

Climax: The highest point of action in your work.

Conflict: Two or more forces grappling with an issue.

Content editing: Sometimes referred to as developmental editing, this involves a review of a manuscript for character development and large-scale issues like flow, plotting, and the arc of the story.

Contest judge: A knowledgeable writer or editor who judges entries in a contest.

Copy edit: A review of a draft or a manuscript for grammar, punctuation, and spelling errors and suggested corrections.

Creative nonfiction: Memoirs, personal essays, articles, and books that take an event and use creative writing techniques to immerse the reader.

Denouement: The wrap-up, ending, or resolution of the story.

Developmental editing: Review of a manuscript or draft for character development and larger-scale issues.

Dialect/Vernacular: Language associated with a specific region or group. Use sparingly.

Dialogue: Conversation between two or more people in written form, such as a book, play, or movie.

Glossary of Terms

Dialogue tags: Notations or phrases used to precede or follow written dialogue that show which character is speaking.

Dual time/split time technique: Two or more timelines where the plot lines intermingle.

Early readers: Books for children ages two through third grade with no more than one hundred words.

Edit: A review of a draft or a manuscript for errors and provides suggested improvements.

Emotion: By showing readers the character's emotions, readers relate to how the characters react to issues.

Essay: Essays are a snapshot and are limited to one or two scenes. They address one point, something close to your heart, through a personal experience or personal observation.

Exposition: The introduction of characters, setting, and the ultimate conflict. It is the opposite of action, as it is telling readers something, not showing them.

Fair use: Judge-created doctrine in United States law that allows a "limited use of copyrighted material" without having permission.

Flash fiction: Short fiction, typically a few hundred words.

Flashback: A memory brought up in time to the story you're telling.

Genre: A category in writing characterized by similarities in style and form or subject, such as Mystery, Suspense, or Romance.

Glossary of Terms

Hero: A main character who is ethical, with moral attributes.

Imagery: Painting pictures with words to evoke a creative response in the reader.

Inner conflict: Conflicts that occur entirely within a character.

Inspirational writing: Writing usually associated with the spiritual. Works that motivate and move people.

Internalization: A writing technique that makes a character's internal thoughts knowable to readers.

Journalism: The profession of gathering, recording, verifying, and writing information related to public importance for newspapers, magazines, news broadcasts, or news websites.

Libel: Knowingly publishing a false statement or statements damaging to a person's reputation.

Line edit: An in-depth, line-by-line edit that checks for word choice, sentence structure, and fact-checking, as well as punctuation, usage, grammar, and spelling.

Linear storytelling: Chronological storytelling.

MacGuffin: An object or a device that triggers the plot.

Memoir: A historical account or biography written from a personal perspective or a special source or learned subject.

Microfiction: Short stories with word counts of fifty words or fewer.

Middle-grade fiction: Books written to appeal to children eight- to twelve-years-old. Typically, these novels run about 20,000 to 50,000 words.

Nonfiction: Writing based upon facts, actual events, and real people.

Novel: A fiction narrative of book length relaying character and action in a sequence of events. Typically, a novel is 75,000 to 90,000 words.

Novella: A fiction narrative shorter than a novel but longer than most short stories. Typically, a novella word count runs from 20,000 to 50,000 words.

One sheet: A single-page document that summarizes a product. In the literary world, it is a summary or showcase of a manuscript with the goal for the manuscript to be published.

Pacing: The flow or rhythm of your story. There needs to be an ebb and flow that is natural, but not boring.

Perspective: The narrator's view of the characters, events, and setting.

Picture book: A book for children from birth to third grade with a word count of less than five hundred. Pictures or sketches drive the story.

Pitch or Pitches: A concise, memorable statement or two about the manuscript or work you wish to publish. A short sales pitch for your work.

Plagiarism: *Random House College Dictionary* defines this as "the appropriation or imitation of the language, ideas, and thoughts of another author and representation of them as one's original work."

Plot: The story told in a series of scenes that develops and unfolds through a period of time and portrays a meaning.

Plot point: An incident or action that directly impacts what happens next in a story.

Point of view: The narrator of a piece of work, telling the story from their perspective, as in the narrator's voice.

Privacy laws: These laws deal with regulating, storing, and using personally identifiable information, such as healthcare information. They also apply to writers in that privacy extends to rights granted by the public. The public has protection from being examined and scrutinized by others in person or in print. These laws apply differently to public figures than private figures. No federal law at the time of this publication protects a celebrities' right to privacy.

Public domain: In copyright law, it is a term that means the ownership of the works has passed from the original creator to the public.

Publisher: A person or company that prepares and issues books, journals, music, and other works for sale.

Query letter: A communication, often via email, sent to magazine editors, newspapers, literary agents, and publishing houses that pitches an author's article idea or book.

Red herrings: Clues sprinkled through most mystery and suspense works that are misleading or distracting to the reader.

Glossary of Terms

Rising action: When action (and tension) builds because of a conflict, which is also building.

Scene break symbol: A symbol showing the end of a scene using three hashtags (###).

Screenwriting: Scripts for movies that include instructions and scene directions.

Setting: The place or surroundings where something happens.

Short fiction: Typically, short fiction is 1,000 words to less than 10,000 words.

Story arc/narrative arc: The chronological plot of a novel or story. It is the direction a storyline takes as it unfolds for the reader.

Storyboarding: A technique using tools such as note cards, whiteboards, sticky notes, or software, to plan and plot your story.

Structure: The design or the bones of the story; the organization or sequence of the plot, characters, and themes.

Subplot: Lessor threads associated with the main plot that give additional dimensions by adding interesting storylines for readers.

Theme: The universal idea, message, or central element explored throughout a book.

Time-slip: A timeline that uses different time eras that are not time travel, and the plot lines of the differing eras don't intermingle.

Glossary of Terms

Time travel: When a character or characters physically move into a different time, either forward, backward, or both, by some type of magical or scientific happenstance.

Viewpoint character: The character who is narrating the scene, the story, or complete work. Often referred to as the POV (point of view) character.

Writing conferences: Meetings of literary professionals that can be regional, national, or international. Attendees include published and unpublished authors, editors, literary agents, and publishers.

Writing organizations and societies: These are professional organizations of authors, artists, literary agents, and publishers dedicated to educating and supporting literature often centered around a specific genre.

Young adult fiction: Books written to appeal to a young adult or teenage reader. Topics are heavier and have more adult themes than children's literature. Typically, 40,000 to 75,000 words.

BIBLIOGRAPHY

Allen, Moira Anderson. *Starting Your Career as a Freelance Writer*. Allworth Press, 2003.

Apple, Linda. *Writing Life: Your Stories Matter!* Birdsong Publishing, 2014.

Arkansas Writers' Conference. *Winning Writers' Waltz, an Anthology of Prize-Winning Creative Writing*. Writing Our World Publishing, 2021.

Associated Press. *The Associated Press Stylebook*, Basic Books, a member of the Perseus Books Group, 2004.

Ball, David. *Backwards & Forwards: A Technical Manual for Reading Plays*. Southern Illinois University Press, 1983.

Bernhardt, William. *Story Structure. The Key to Successful Fiction*. Red Sneaker Press. 2013.

Bickham, Jack M. *The 38 Most Common Fiction Writing Mistakes (And How To Avoid Them)*. Publisher Writer's Digest Books, 1997.

Bruno, Beth. *How to Enter and Win Book Award Contests*. www.book-editing.com/book-awards-contests/

Cappon, Rene J. *The Associated Press Guide to News Writing, Fourth Edition*. Peterson's Publishing, 2019.

Dobson, Melanie, Smith, Morgan Tarpley. *A Split in Time: How to Write Dual Timeline, Split Time and Time-Slip Fiction*. Ink Map Press, 2020.

Engler, James. *Six Figure Freelancing: The Writer's Guide to Making More Money*. Random House Reference, 2005.

Evanovich, Janet with Ina Yalof. *How I Write: Secrets of a Bestselling Author*. St. Martin's Press, 2006.

Fulkerson, Linda, Hope Bolinger, Rowena Kwo, and Carrie Schmidt. *Getting Past the Publishing Gatekeepers: Winning the Hearts of Agents, Publishers, Editors, and Readers*. Scrivenings Press, 2022.

Garrett, Del. *A Writer's 'How To' Plan Plotting, Writing, and Self-Publishing your Next Book*. Raven's Inn Press. 2017.

Hudson, Robert. *The Christian Writer's Manual of Style, Fourth Edition*. Zondervan Academic, 2016.

JAMA Network Editors. *American Medical Association Manual of Style*, 11th Edition. Oxford University Press, 2020.

Leonard, Elmore. *Elmore Leonard's 10 Rules of Writing*. William Morrow, an imprint of HarperCollins Publishers. 2007.

Miclea, Lynn. *Grammar Tips & Tools: Tantalizing Tidbits to Improve Your Writing*. Independently published, 2021.

McCarthy, Zoe M. *Tailor Your Fiction Manuscript in 30 Days*. Sonfire Media, LLC. 2019.

Bibliography

Mitchell, Margaret. *Gone with the Wind*. The Macmillan Company. 1936.

Plotnik, Author. *Spunk & Bite: A Writer's Guide to Punchier, More Engaging Language & Style*. Random House Reference. 2005.

Prose, Francine. *Reading Like A Writer: A Guide for People Who Love Books and For Those Who Want to Write Them*. Harper Perennial. 2007.

Random House Webster's College Dictionary, Random House Reference, 2000.

Sakaduski, Nancy. *How to Write Winning Short Stories: A practical guide to writing stories that win contests and get selected for publication*. Cat and Mouse Press, 2015.

Selgin, Peter. *179 Ways to Save a Novel*. Writer's Digest Books, 2010.

Stein, Sol. *Stein on Writing*. St. Martin's Press, 2000

Stowe, Harriett Beecher. *Uncle Tom's Cabin*. Original publication date, 1852.

Suber, Howard. *The Power of Film*. Michael Wise Productions, 2006.

The Writer. A magazine published by Madavor Media, founded in 1887.

Truss, Lynne. *Eats, Shoots & Leaves: The Zero Tolerance Approach to Punctuation*. Gotham Books, 2003.

United States. *United States Government Publishing Office Style Manual*, Federal Government Publishing, 2020.

University of Chicago Press Editorial Staff. *The Chicago Manual of Style*, 17th Edition. University of Chicago Press, 2017.

Vogler, Christopher. *The Writer's Journey 2nd Edition, Mythic Structure for Writers*. Michael Wiese Productions. 1998.

Wheat, Carolyn. *How to Write Killer Fiction*. Perseverance Press, John Daniel & Company. 2003.

Writer's Digest. A magazine. Active Interest Media, founded in 1920.

Writer's Digest Handbook of Magazine Article Writing, Writer's Digest Books, 2005.

Writer's Market Guides. (*Writer's Market, Guide to Literary Agents, Children's Writer's & Illustrator's Market, Novel & Short Story Writer's Market*, and *Poet's Market*) Published annually by Penguin Random House.

www.copyright.gov. Website maintained by the U. S. Government for more information regarding copyright laws and the Fair Use Doctrine.

Zuckerman, Albert. *Writing the Blockbuster Novel*. Writer's Digest Books. 1994.

ACKNOWLEDGMENTS

I am indebted to Linda Fulkerson for believing writers will want to learn the steps to prize-winning works. In addition, I am grateful for all my friends who have judged contests and shared their experiences to make this book possible.

ABOUT THE AUTHOR

Ellen E. Withers is a multiple award-winning freelance writer and retired insurance fraud investigator. She is proud to have written *Magic Words: Enchant Judges & Conjure Contest Wins for Novels, Short Fiction and Nonfiction*. She hopes this book will help other writers accomplish their goals for winning contests.

Her professional writing career began in 2003 as a freelance contributor to the *Arkansas Democrat-Gazette*. For ten years, Ellen was editor of an international magazine, *SIU Today*, for insurance fraud investigators, and she remains on their editorial committee. She has written for Life in Chenal Magazine since 2006.

Ellen's mystery dual-time series, Show Me Mysteries, is set in her picturesque hometown of Mexico, Missouri. Scrivenings Press published *Show Me Betrayal*, the first book of the series, in 2023. Scrivenings Press published *Show Me Deceit* in 2024.

In a celebration of Christmas traditions, Ellen is one of three contributors to a Christmas novella collection titled *A Gift for All Time*, released in 2023 from Scrivenings Press. Her novella, "Carving Out Love," is the middle of the three chronological stories related to Christmas.

Other publishing credits include short stories in over twenty anthologies. One of her short stories garnered a nomination for the prestigious Pushcart Prize in the published short story category.

Ellen is an officer of the Pioneer Branch of the National League of American Pen Women and a board member of the Arkansas Writers Conference. She's a member of White County Creative Writers, American Christian Fiction Writers, and Sisters in Crime (SIC). She is also a member of two chapters of the SIC, Tornado Alley, and Upstate South Carolina chapter.

She enjoys spending time with her family, traveling the world with her adventurous friends, and performing with Top of the Rock Chorus, a Sweet Adeline chorus in central Arkansas.

ALSO BY ELLEN E. WITHERS

Show Me Betrayal by Ellen E. Withers

Show Me Mysteries - Book One

Double-finalist in the American Christian Fiction Writers Carol Awards

Two deaths occur decades apart. Is it possible these deaths are related? What motivates a killer, who got away with murder sixty years ago, to kill again? Was it uncontrollable rage or the hope of silencing someone who fit all the puzzle pieces together and deduced who committed the crime?

Set in the picturesque town of Mexico, Missouri, *Show Me Betrayal* takes flight in words and emotions of rich characters woven together into a story you won't want to put down.

Get your copy here:
https://scrivenings.link/showmebetrayal

Show Me Deceit

Show Me Mysteries - Book Two

Present Day: Liesl Schrader is once again involved in death investigations. A body is discovered inside a charitable museum where Liesl serves on the board of directors. She and her best friend Nicole are drawn into a police theft investigation stemming from the death at the museum.

When Liesl and Nicole uncover a set of historic bones, questions arise. Are they related to the Civil War-era encampment in their town? The unit, commanded by General Pope, guarded one of the biggest supply chains of the Union Army—the railroad lines located in Mexico, Missouri, throughout the war. Was this a battlefield death, or was it murder? Surrounded on all sides by Southern sympathizers, did the Rebels kill this Union soldier?

1862: United States Army Lieutenant Cormac O'Malley has a problem. He knows there is a Rebel spy in his camp, and he needs proof of the spy to save the lives of Union soldiers. He has no choice but to work with his sweetheart from town, Enid Connelly, and her local friends to uncover the proof. Are they trustworthy and loyal to the Union in a state divided between North and South? Can he reveal the identity of the spy before the spy can silence him—possibly forever?

Take a walk through time with *Show Me Deceit*, book two of the Show Me Mystery Series. The mysteries are set in Mexico, Missouri, where death encompasses two eras—Civil War and contemporary times. Liesl, Nicole, and Detective Kurt Hunter, have previously put a killer behind bars. Now they must combine their skills again to stop the plunder of local charities and solve the mystery of a Union soldier's death. Can Liesl and Kurt work together again as friends, putting aside their former romance, to solve these mysteries?

Get your copy here:

https://scrivenings.link/showmedeceit

A Collection of Three Christmas Novellas

by Tonya B. Ashley, Jenny Carlisle, and

Ellen E. Withers

A beautiful hand-carved nativity set travels from its original home in Germany to a riverboat in Van Buren, Arkansas, in the mid-1840s, then to Mexico, Missouri, at the beginning of the American Civil War. More than a century later, it resurfaces in a tiny town in the Arkansas River Valley.

Three stories tell of the impact this treasure has on the families who own it. God's love survives tragedy, turmoil, and even abandonment. His love is the gift for all, for all time.

Get your copy here:

https://scrivenings.link/agiftforalltime

YOU MAY ALSO LIKE

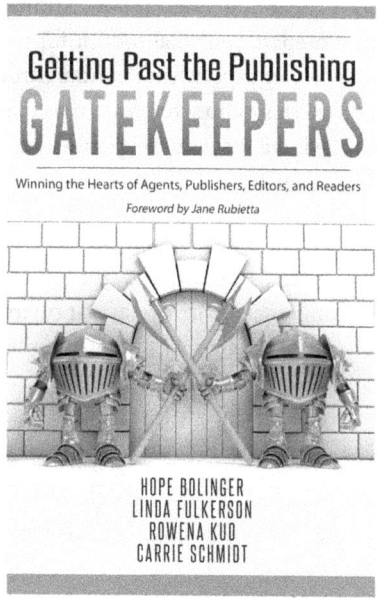

Getting Past the Publishing Gatekeepers: Winning the Hearts of Agents, Publishers, Editors, and Readers

There are four "gatekeepers" in publishing: Agents, publishers, editors, and readers. So how do authors win their hearts?

Agents

Love 'em or hate 'em, agents are a necessity in the publishing industry. Former agent Hope Bolinger will walk you through what makes a good agent, how to win them over, and how to break up with a bad agent.

Publishers

Becoming a published author can be one of the most exciting and rewarding events in your life. However, understanding (and enduring) the publication process can be one of the most frightening and frustrating. Publisher Linda Fulkerson offers tips and tidbits that can help alleviate your angst and bypass the bafflements.

Editors

On the road to publication, editors can be your greatest challenges and your best friends. This section focuses on how editing before submission can better prepare your manuscript for presentation to publishers and what you can expect from editors throughout the life of your work. Rowena Kuo shares how to create that masterpiece manuscript that can navigate through the publishing process, pre-contract to post-publication.

Readers

Once all the other gates have been opened, the author must now win the hearts of readers. Influencer Carrie Schmidt offers practical tips and behind-the-scenes insights that will show you the path to getting your book in front of new readers–and keeping them for the long haul. Your story matters. Here's how to get it read.

Get your copy here:

https://scrivenings.link/gatekeepers

Stay up-to-date on your favorite books and authors with our free e-newsletters.

ScriveningsPress.com

www.ingramcontent.com/pod-product-compliance
Lightning Source LLC
Chambersburg PA
CBHW051546020426
42333CB00016B/2121